ANN M. MARTIN

THE BABY-SITTERS CLUB

MALLORY AND THE TROUBLE WITH TWINS

A GRAPHIC NOVEL BY

ARLEY NOPRA

WITH COLOR BY BRADEN LAMB AND JASON CAFFOE

An Imprint of

SCHOLASTIC

This book is for the Palladinos
and the Ameses, especially Kathy

A. M. M.

For everyone on the
exciting journey of self-discovery

A. N.

Library of Congress Control Number: 2024935920

ISBN 978-93-5954-827-2

Printed in India at Polykam Offset New Delhi 110028
This reprint edition, March 2025

Edited by Cassandra Pelham Fulton and Megan Peace
Creative Director: Phil Falco
Publisher: David Saylor

CHAPTER 1
KINDERGARTEN BABY, STICK YOUR HEAD IN GRAVY! WASH IT OFF WITH APPLESAUCE AND SHOW IT TO THE NAVY!
MOMMY. MAKE HIM STOP!
NICHOLAS PIKE, THIS IS SUPPOSED TO BE FUN. WE ARE GOING TO WASHINGTON MALL WHERE EACH OF YOU KIDS IS GOING TO GET A NEW PAIR OF SHOES.

YOU WANT NEW SHOES, DON'T YOU?
YES...
THEN APOLOGIZE TO YOUR SISTER.

SORRY, CLAIRE.

KINDERGARTEN BABY.

AUGH!
HI. I'M MALLORY PIKE.
GRRR!
ALL RIGHT. CALM DOWN, BOTH OF YOU.
I'M ELEVEN AND THE OLDEST OF EIGHT CHILDREN.
MALL TRIP SEATING PLAN
BYRON
ADAM
JORDAN
Triplets in the back so they won't bother anyone
Row #3
CLAIRE
ME
NICKY
I MUST sit between them, they WILL argue
Row #2
Margo feels less carsick here
MARGO
VANESSA
Vanessa is happiest day-dreaming by the window
Row #1
WHEN IT CAME TO KIDS -- MY BROTHERS AND SISTERS, OR ANY OTHERS -- I WAS PRETTY SMART. I FIGURED OUT THE SEATING ARRANGEMENT FOR OUR OUTING TO THE MALL.

WE'RE HERE!
YAAAY!
WASHINGTON MALL
NEW SHOES! NEW SHOES! NEW SHOES!
ALL RIGHT! I WANT SNEAKERS, AND THEY HAVE TO BE ADIDAS OR NIKE. EITHER ONE!
OH, YOU ARE SO COOL, NICK.

HAPPY BEAR
Bloomwear
Pixels
THE MALL WAS LIKE ANOTHER WORLD.
I WANTED TO CHECK OUT ALL THE STUFF I WASN'T ALLOWED TO HAVE YET.
SHOES FIRST.

ANTOINETTE'S
SHOE TREE
SALE
SALE
SALE
30%
OFF
WHAT ON EARTH IS
A SHOE TREE?

SO COOL.

MALLORY, I'M BUYING YOU THESE LOAFERS.

THEY'RE SO PRACTICAL. THEY GO WITH ALMOST EVERYTHING YOU OWN AND THEY'LL LAST AT LEAST A YEAR.
WHEN YOU WERE A PARENT OF EIGHT CHILDREN, YOU HAD TO THINK ABOUT THESE THINGS.

sigh...
...OKAY.
GREAT!
ANTOINE
SHOE TR

YOU ALL HAVE ONE HOUR TO EXPLORE. MAKE SURE TO MEET AT THIS EXACT SPOT, OKAY?
GOT IT!
CAN WE PLEEAAASE GO WITH YOU, MAL?
YOU DO FUN THINGS!
ALL RIGHT.
TODAY, WE'RE GOING TO WATCH PEOPLE HAVE THEIR EARS PIERCED.
COOL!
Ear Piercing Boutique

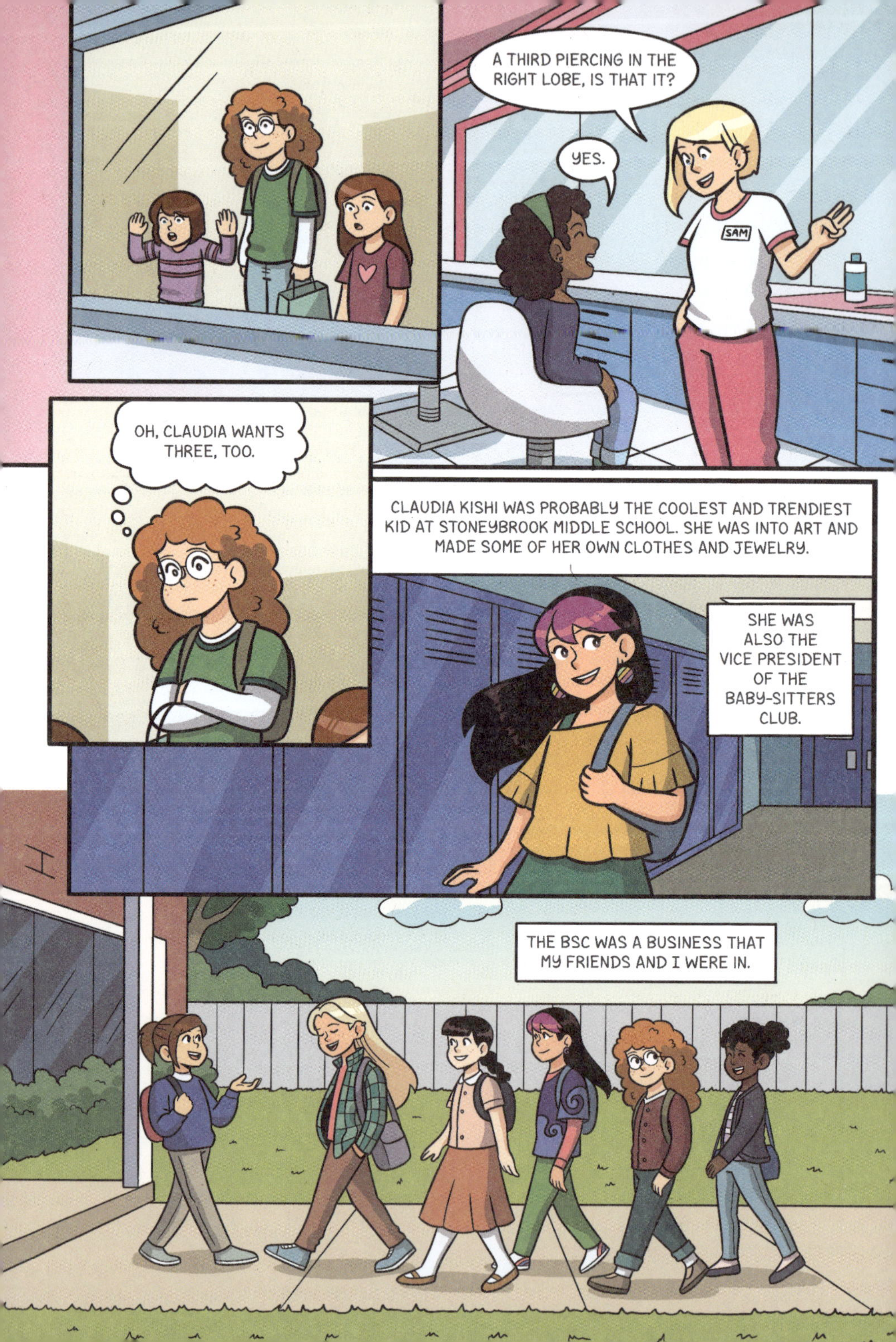
A THIRD PIERCING IN THE RIGHT LOBE, IS THAT IT?
YES.
SAM
OH, CLAUDIA WANTS THREE, TOO.
CLAUDIA KISHI WAS PROBABLY THE COOLEST AND TRENDIEST KID AT STONEYBROOK MIDDLE SCHOOL. SHE WAS INTO ART AND MADE SOME OF HER OWN CLOTHES AND JEWELRY.
SHE WAS ALSO THE VICE PRESIDENT OF THE BABY-SITTERS CLUB.
THE BSC WAS A BUSINESS THAT MY FRIENDS AND I WERE IN.

THE PRESIDENT WAS KRISTY THOMAS. SHE WAS LOUD, OUTGOING, AND FULL OF GREAT IDEAS.

OUR SECRETARY WAS MARY ANNE SPIER. SHE WAS SHY, SENSITIVE, AND SENTIMENTAL.

DAWN SCHAFER WAS THE CLUB'S TREASURER. SHE WAS LAID-BACK AND ADORED SUNSHINE AND WARM WEATHER. A REAL INDIVIDUAL.

JESSI RAMSEY AND I WERE THE YOUNGEST MEMBERS OF THE CLUB AND WERE JUNIOR OFFICERS. JESSI WAS A VERY TALENTED BALLET DANCER.

SHE WAS ALSO MY BEST FRIEND! WE SHARED A LOT OF THE SAME INTERESTS, LIKE READING.
WE BOTH WANTED PIERCED EARS, TRENDIER CLOTHES, AND DECENT HAIRCUTS AS WELL...BUT OUR PARENTS TREATED US LIKE BABIES.

WILL JESSI AND I GET TO SIT IN THAT CHAIR ONE DAY?
MAYBE WHEN WE'RE SEVENTY-TWO?
LIZ
READY?
READY.
POKE
PRESS
AUGHH!

I THINK I'M GOING TO BARF...
SHE GOT A **HOLE** PUT IN HER **EAR!**
YOU ARE NOT GOING TO BARF. YOU ARE **NOT.**
IS EVERYTHING ALL RIGHT OUT THERE?
SORRY!
YUCK!
BLEGH!
?

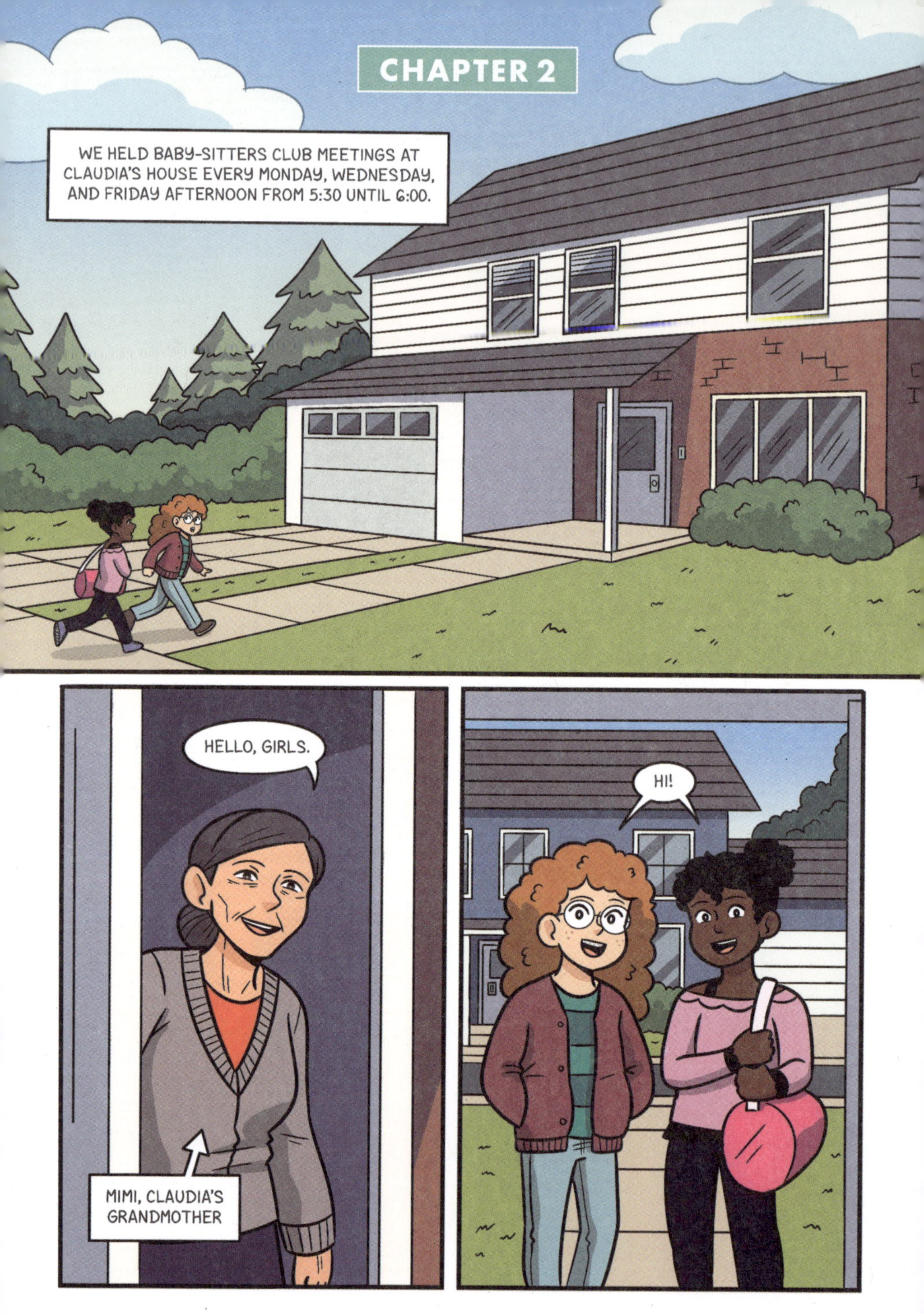

CHAPTER 2

WE HELD BABY-SITTERS CLUB MEETINGS AT CLAUDIA'S HOUSE EVERY MONDAY, WEDNESDAY, AND FRIDAY AFTERNOON FROM 5:30 UNTIL 6:00.

ARE WE THE LAST TO ARRIVE?
YES. BUT YOU'RE NOT LATE. IT ISN'T 5:30 YET.
THAT'S A RELIEF.

YOU WILL FIND A SURPRISE IN CLAUDIA'S ROOM.

HI, EVERYONE.

THERE REALLY WAS A SURPRISE.
HELLO! LOOK WHO CAME TO THE MEETING.
IT WAS LOGAN BRUNO, MARY ANNE'S BOYFRIEND. HE DIDN'T USUALLY COME TO MEETINGS BECAUSE HE WAS AN ASSOCIATE MEMBER. HE TOOK ON JOBS IF NONE OF US WERE FREE.
HI.
SHANNON KILBOURNE WAS OUR OTHER ASSOCIATE MEMBER. SHE WAS A FRIEND OF KRISTY'S.
HEYYY.
WE HADN'T EXPECTED TO SEE A BOY AT THE MEETING.

OKAY, ORDER! ORDER!
LET'S GET STARTED.

WE CONDUCTED
BUSINESS AS USUAL.

THIRTY MINUTES LATER
munch munch
munch munch
munch munch
munch munch
RING
RING RING
GULP
I'LL GET IT!
NO! NO! MMPH!

MMPHH, MMPHH, MMPHH.
OUR CLIENTS AREN'T USED TO A BOY ANSWERING THE PHONE. NOT THAT THERE'S ANYTHING WRONG WITH IT! I JUST DON'T WANT TO TAKE ANYONE BY SURPRISE.
RING
HELLO. BABY-SITTERS CLUB!
YES? MRS. ARNOLD?
OKAY, I SEE.
I'LL GET BACK TO YOU. BYE.
THAT WAS MRS. ARNOLD, THE MOTHER OF THE TWINS.

THE TWINS?

OH, YOU HAVEN'T MET THEM YET.
THE CLUB HAS SAT FOR THEM A COUPLE TIMES. THE ARNOLDS HAVE TWIN DAUGHTERS. THEY'RE SEVEN. MARILYN AND CAROLYN.

MARILYN AND CAROLYN?!
DON'T TELL ME -- THEY'RE IDENTICAL?
RIGHT DOWN TO THE BUCKLES ON THEIR SHOES.

THEY'RE NICE, THOUGH. I MEAN, THEY CAN'T HELP HOW THEIR PARENTS DRESS THEM.

ANYWAY, MRS. ARNOLD NEEDS A STEADY SITTER, SOMEONE WHO CAN TAKE CARE OF THE TWINS TWO AFTERNOONS A WEEK FOR THE NEXT EIGHT WEEKS.

THAT'S A
BIG JOB.

YEAH. THERE'S SOME SORT OF FUNDRAISING PROJECT AT STONEYBROOK ELEMENTARY. MRS. ARNOLD IS IN CHARGE OF IT, SO SHE'LL BE PRETTY BUSY.

SHE WANTS SOMEONE EVERY TUESDAY AND THURSDAY AFTERNOON FROM 3:30 TO 6:00.
BOY, THIS IS A TOUGH ONE.

JESSI, YOU'RE OUT, OBVIOUSLY.
YUP. BALLET CLASS.

I BETTER BE OUT, TOO. THERE'S A CHANCE MY ART CLASSES WILL SWITCH TO THURSDAYS.

I'VE GOT SEVERAL JOBS LINED UP FOR TUESDAYS AND THURSDAYS.

ME TOO.

HMMM...
LOOKS LIKE I CAN'T TAKE IT, EITHER.

I THOUGHT ABOUT THE MONEY I'D EARN IF I TOOK ON THE JOB.
I COULD GET MY HAIR CUT AND EARS PIERCED IF I FOUND A WAY TO CONVINCE MOM AND DAD TO LET ME.

MALLORY, WOULD YOU LIKE THE JOB?
ME?

I'LL TAKE IT!
PERFECT.

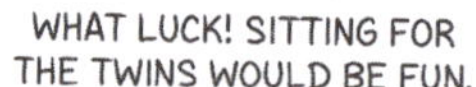
WHAT LUCK! SITTING FOR THE TWINS WOULD BE FUN.

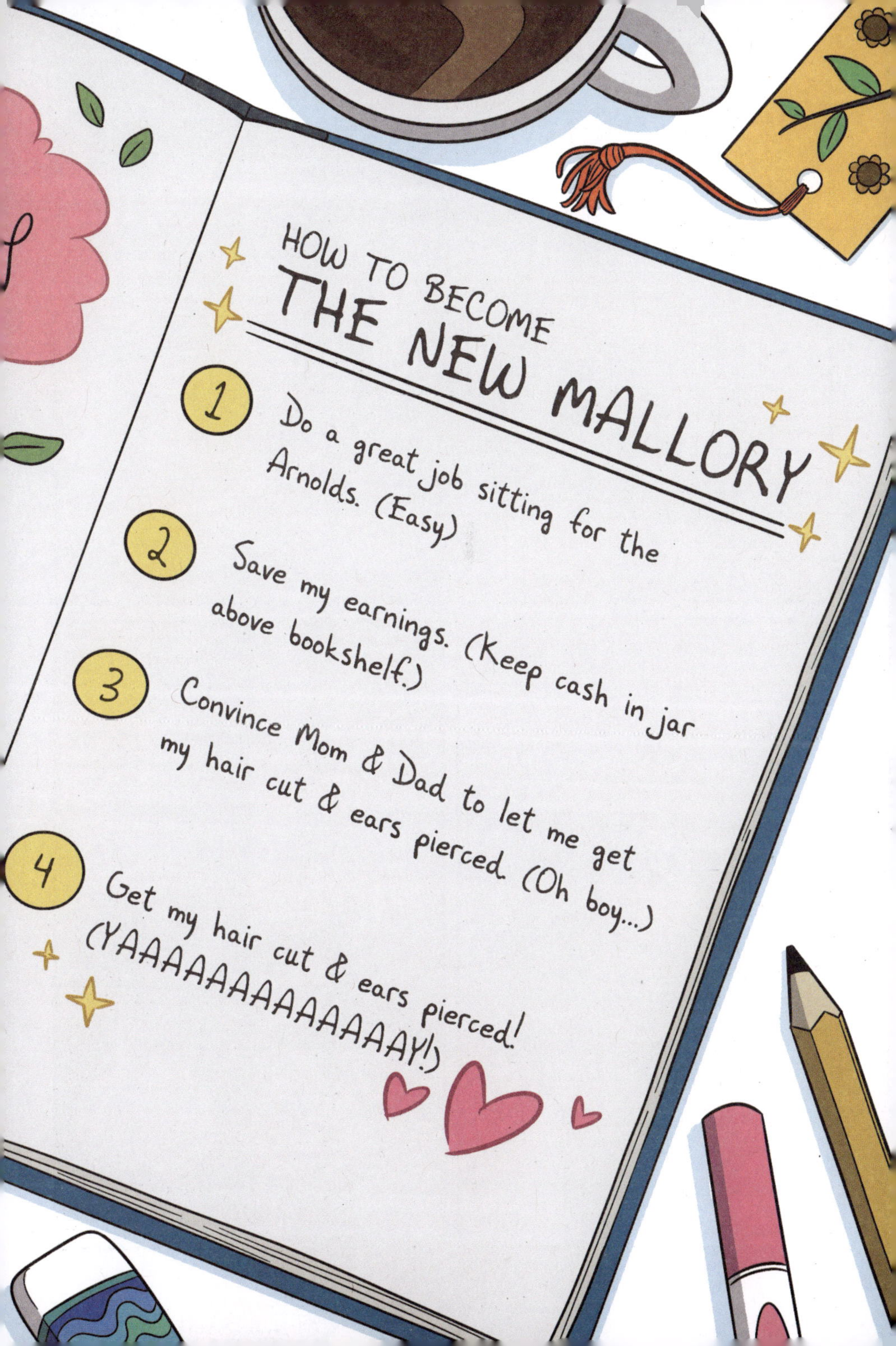
HOW TO BECOME
THE NEW MALLORY
1 Do a great job sitting for the Arnolds. (Easy)
2 Save my earnings. (Keep cash in jar above bookshelf.)
3 Convince Mom & Dad to let me get my hair cut & ears pierced. (Oh boy...)
4 Get my hair cut & ears pierced! (YAAAAAAAAAAAAAY!)

CHAPTER 3

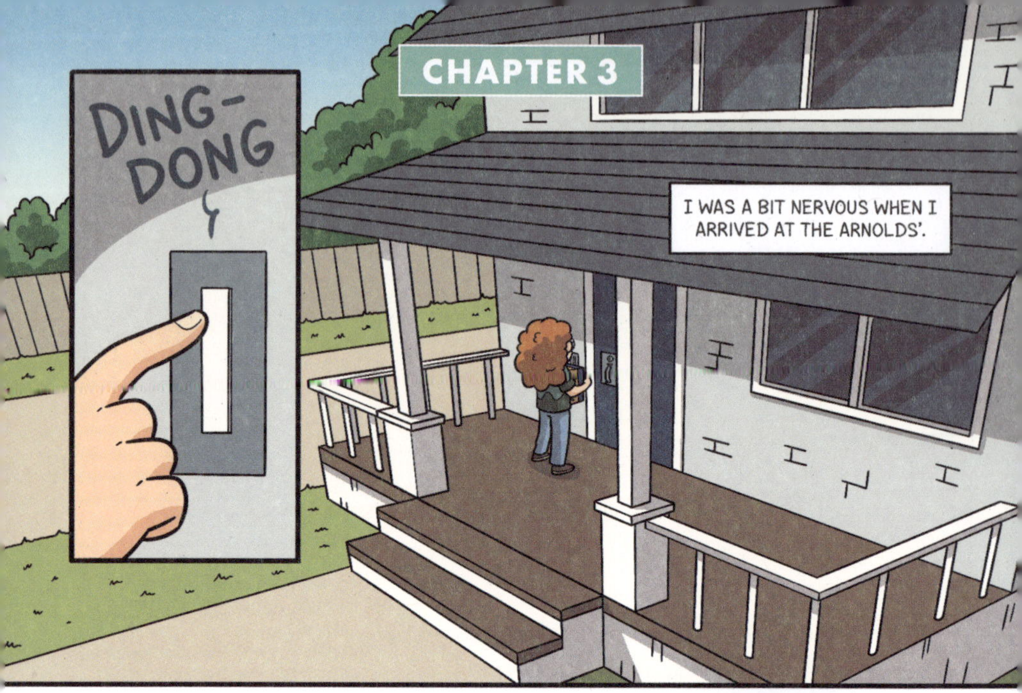

DING-DONG

I WAS A BIT NERVOUS WHEN I ARRIVED AT THE ARNOLDS'.

BABY-SITTING FOR A NEW CLIENT ALWAYS REMINDED ME OF THE FIRST DAY OF SCHOOL. I HAD A VAGUE IDEA OF WHAT I WAS GETTING INTO BUT DIDN'T KNOW THE SPECIFICS.

I KNEW THEY WERE IDENTICAL BUT THEY LOOKED **SO** ALIKE IT WAS AS IF I WAS SEEING ONE KID AND HER REFLECTION IN THE MIRROR.
MOOOOOM!
MALLORY IS HERE!

M
C
LUCKILY, THEY HAD IDENTIFICATION BRACELETS.

WHAT'S THAT?
IT'S A KID-KIT, CAROLYN.

DO YOU LIKE KID-KITS? THIS ONE HAS SOME GOOD THINGS IN IT.
OH BOY!

HI, MALLORY, I'M MRS. ARNOLD.
MALLORY BROUGHT TOYS FOR US!
THAT'S LOVELY. THE THREE OF YOU ARE OFF TO A HAPPY START.
EMERGENCY PHONE NUMBERS ARE ON THE FRIDGE.
AND PLEASE MAKE SURE THAT MARILYN PRACTICES THE PIANO FOR HALF AN HOUR.
I'LL SEE YOU TWO AT 6:00.

GOOD-BYE, LOVES.
BYE, MOMMY!

CAN WE SEE THE KID-KIT NOW?
SURE, UM...

SQUINT

M

MARILYN.
YAY!
LET'S GO TO OUR ROOM!

WHOA.
BOTH SIDES OF THE ROOM LOOKED EXACTLY THE SAME.
TWO.
TWO.
TWO OF EVERYTHING!

OKAY, HERE YOU GO. I'VE GOT BOOKS TO READ, PUZZLES, JACKS, AND SOME NEW COLORING BOOKS.

I LIKE TO READ.
I LIKE PUZZLES.

I LOVE THIS ONE. HOPE YOU ENJOY IT!
THANKS.

IT'S SPACE-THEMED.
COOL!

AWWW. YOU GUYS ARE SO CUTE!
I WISH I HAD MY CAMERA. YOU LOOK LIKE BOOKENDS!

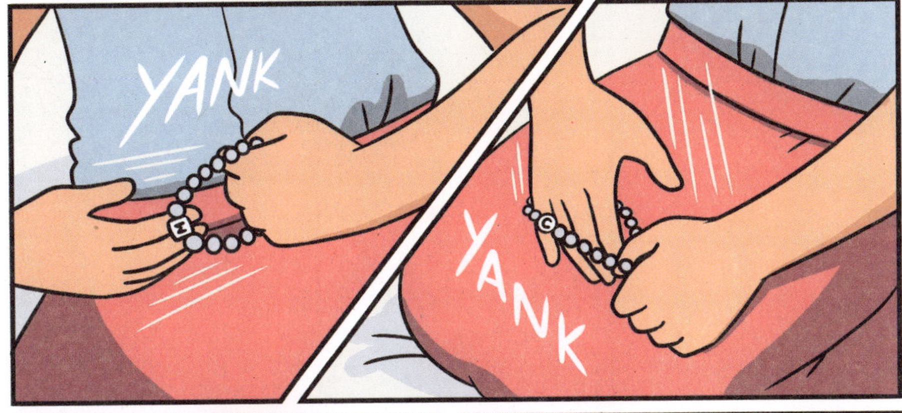
YANK
YANK

BOGGLE.

OOM-BAH.

CHAD POM.
DOVER GLOP.
HUH?
BLIP BLOP!
WHAT ARE YOU TWO DOING?!
YIM TUM!

NOW TELL US APART!
I CANT. YOU DON'T HAVE YOUR BRACELETS ON.
DO YOU LIKE TO BABY-SIT?
YES?
WELL, YOU WON'T LIKE TO SIT FOR US.
HEY!
SPARKLES

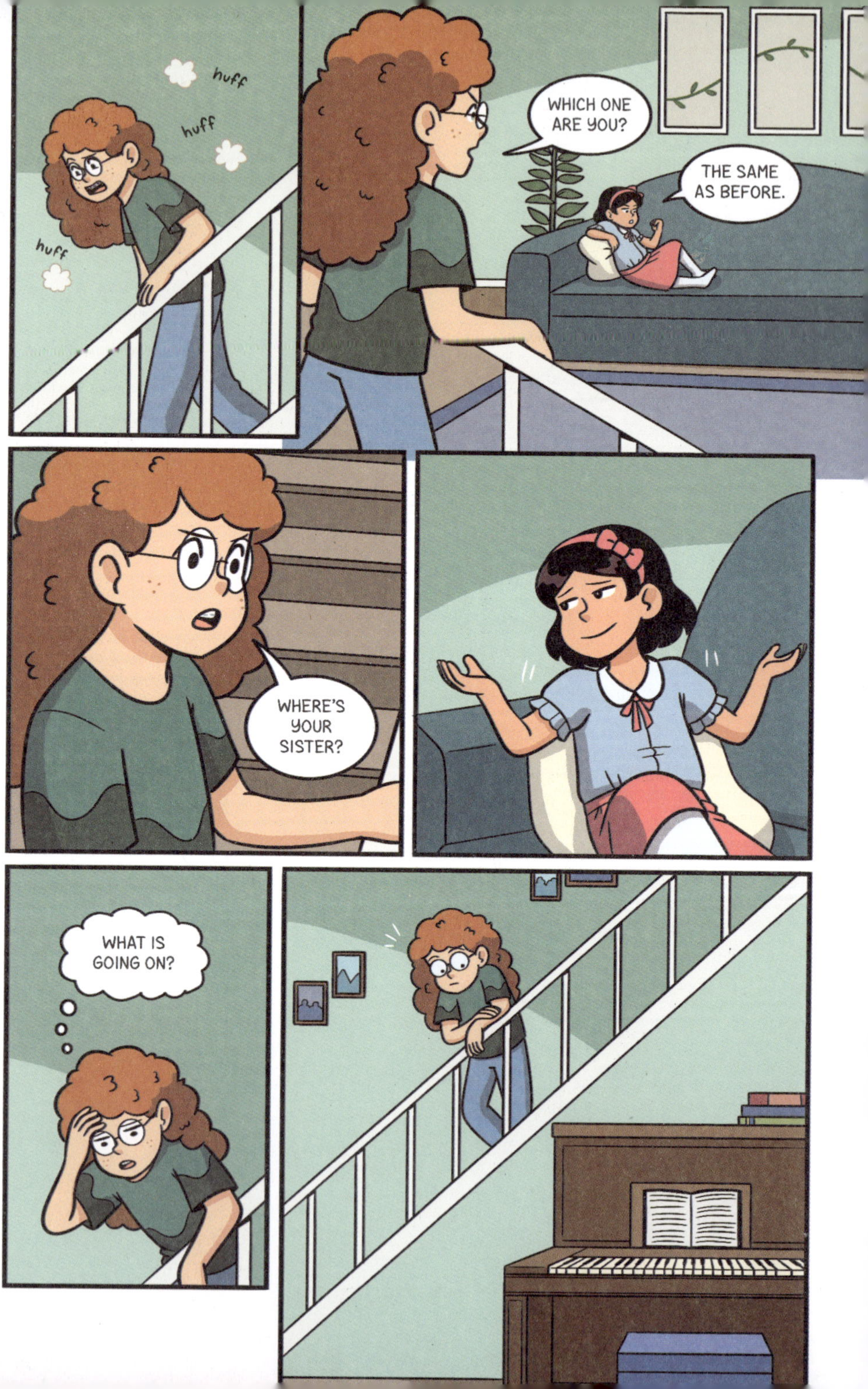

huff
huff
huff
WHICH ONE ARE YOU?
THE SAME AS BEFORE.
WHERE'S YOUR SISTER?

ALL RIGHT.
PRACTICE TIME.
GO AHEAD.
YOU CAN PLAY,
CAN'T YOU?
DUUN
THANK YOU, CAROLYN. NOW
PLEASE TELL YOUR SISTER
IT'S TIME TO PRACTICE.
OKAY...

C
M

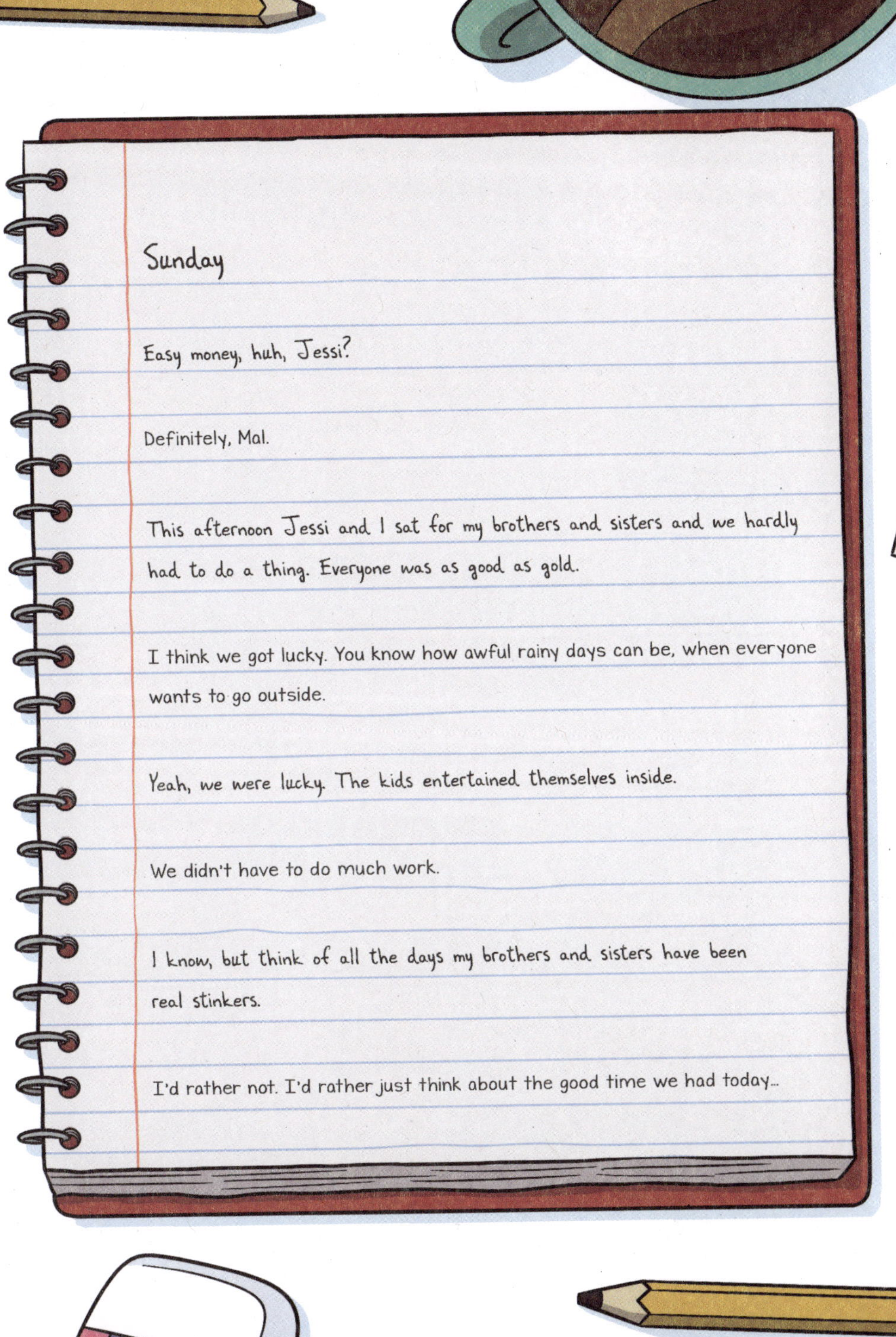
Sunday
Easy money, huh, Jessi?
Definitely, Mal.
This afternoon Jessi and I sat for my brothers and sisters and we hardly had to do a thing. Everyone was as good as gold.
I think we got lucky. You know how awful rainy days can be, when everyone wants to go outside.
Yeah, we were lucky. The kids entertained themselves inside.
We didn't have to do much work.
I know, but think of all the days my brothers and sisters have been real stinkers.
I'd rather not. I'd rather just think about the good time we had today...

CHAPTER 4

IT SURE WAS AN EASY SITTING JOB. FOR ONCE, EVERY ONE OF MY BROTHERS AND SISTERS WAS BUSY AND HAPPY.

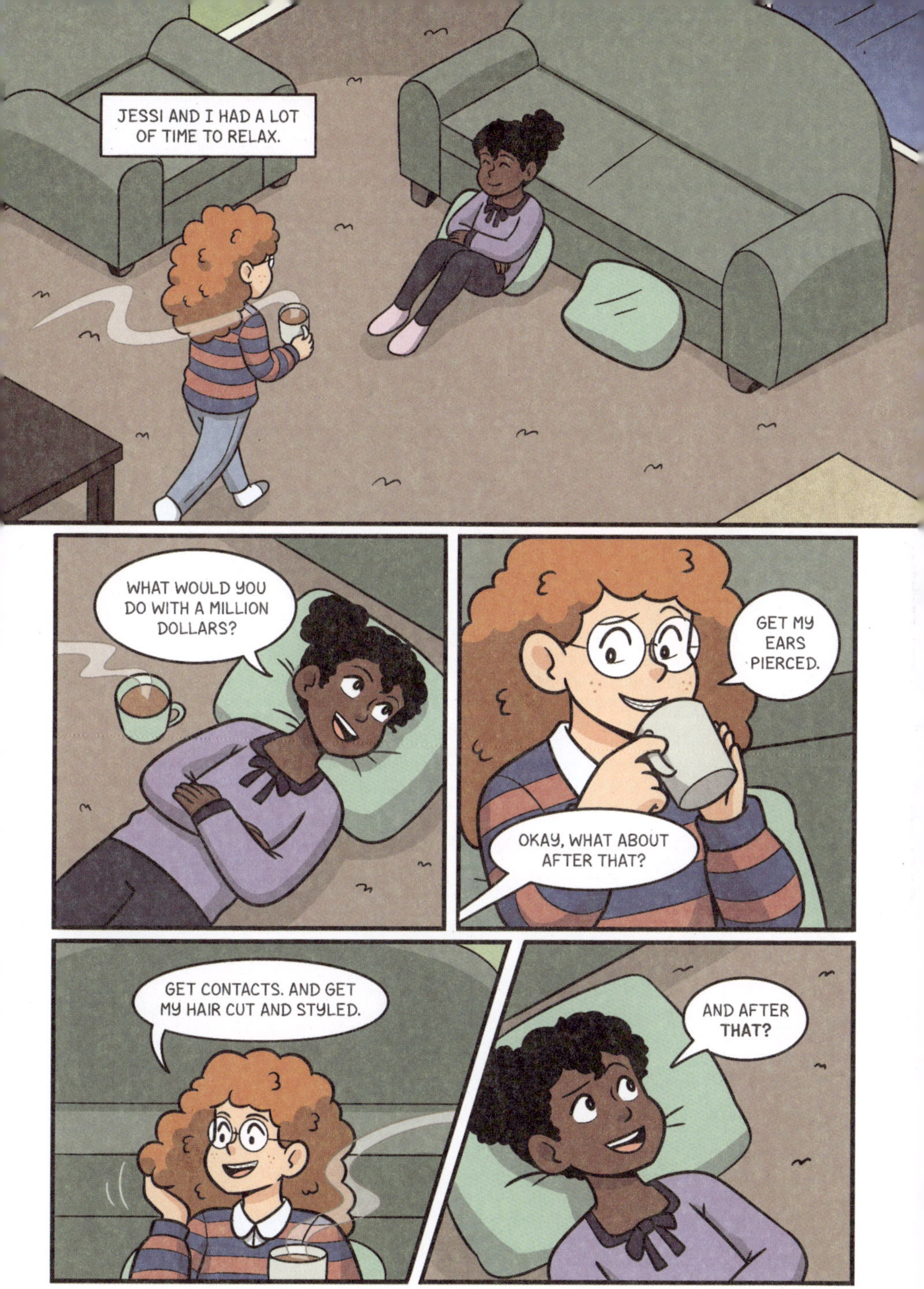

JESSI AND I HAD A LOT OF TIME TO RELAX.

PAY THE ORTHODONTIST TO REMOVE MY BRACES.
ha ha
THEN WHAT?
BUY A NINE-BEDROOM HOUSE FOR MY FAMILY.
SO EACH OF YOU KIDS WOULD HAVE YOUR OWN ROOM?
YES, EXACTLY.

EVEN THE TRIPLETS?

DEFINITELY.

I MEAN, THEY SPEND A LOT OF TIME TOGETHER, BUT THEY ARE DIFFERENT PEOPLE.
THEY HAVE DIFFERENT INTERESTS AND SOMETIMES THEY GET ON EACH OTHER'S NERVES.

IT'S FUNNY. I'VE NEVER HAD TROUBLE TELLING THE TRIPLETS APART. WELL, MAYBE A LITTLE WHEN I FIRST MET THEM.
YEAH. MOST PEOPLE DON'T HAVE ANY TROUBLE.

OKAY, WHAT WOULD **YOU** DO WITH A MILLION BUCKS?

GET MY EARS PIERCED.

ha ha ha ha ha ha ha ha

HA...YOU KNOW...

I FEEL LIKE A BABY BECAUSE MOM AND DAD WON'T LET ME GET MY EARS PIERCED OR MY HAIR CUT OR WEAR COOL CLOTHES.

BUT WHEN I THINK ABOUT IT, MAYBE **THEY'RE** THE BABIES. I MEAN, EAR-PIERCING IS SAFE IF YOU HAVE IT DONE PROFESSIONALLY.
I DON'T THINK YOUR PARENTS -- OR MINE -- ARE BABIES. I KNOW WHAT YOU MEAN, BUT THEY MUST HAVE GOOD REASONS FOR WHAT THEY WILL AND WON'T ALLOW.
WHOSE SIDE ARE YOU ON?
I'M JUST BEING DIPLOMA--
HEY, LOOK! TWINS!
WHAT HAPPENED TO YOUR BOARD GAME?

WE GOT TIRED OF
IT, SO WE DECIDED TO
DO A FASHION SHOW.

CLAIRE
GOT TIRED
OF IT.
SILLY-BILLY-
GOO-GOO.

THIS IS THE FIRST FASHION OF
THE YEAR. IT'S THE TERRIFIC
TWIN OUTFIT.
STUNNING.
SUPERB.

GOTTA
CHANGE!
NEW OUTFIT
COMING UP!

REMEMBER HOW FUN IT USED TO BE TO PRETEND YOU HAD A TWIN?
MAYBE? I DON'T THINK I DID THAT.
OH, BECCA AND I USED TO DO IT ALL THE TIME.
WE'D WEAR MATCHING DRESSES AND TELL EVERYONE WE WERE TWINS. BUT WE'RE THREE YEARS APART SO WE MUST HAVE LOOKED LIKE GOOFBALLS!
I KNOW KRISTY AND KAREN HAVE A MATCHING SISTER OUTFIT THAT --
OKAY! HERE WE ARE AGAIN!
YOU ARE NOW SEEING BEACH FASHION!
IMPRESSIVE.
SMASHING.

BUT YOU KNOW WHAT WOULD MAKE MY LIFE PERFECT?

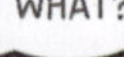

GETTING MY EARS PIERCED AND LOOKING MORE GROWN-UP.
DREAM ON, MAL. DREAM ON.

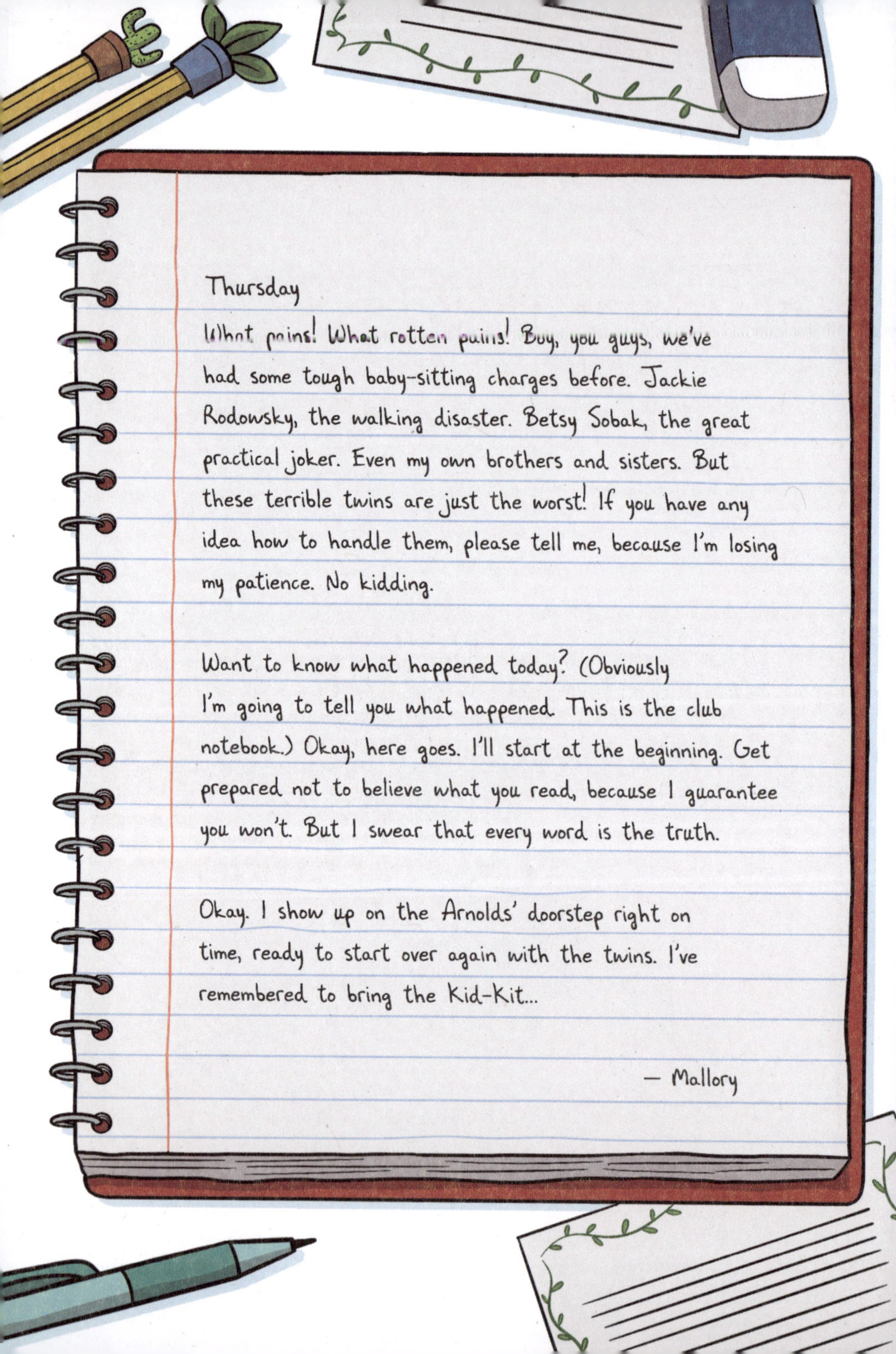

Thursday

What pains! What rotten pains! Boy, you guys, we've had some tough baby-sitting charges before. Jackie Rodowsky, the walking disaster. Betsy Sobak, the great practical joker. Even my own brothers and sisters. But these terrible twins are just the worst! If you have any idea how to handle them, please tell me, because I'm losing my patience. No kidding.

Want to know what happened today? (Obviously I'm going to tell you what happened. This is the club notebook.) Okay, here goes. I'll start at the beginning. Get prepared not to believe what you read, because I guarantee you won't. But I swear that every word is the truth.

Okay. I show up on the Arnolds' doorstep right on time, ready to start over again with the twins. I've remembered to bring the Kid-Kit...

— Mallory

CHAPTER 5

BYE, GIRLS! I'LL BE BACK BEFORE YOU KNOW IT.

REMEMBER TO PRACTICE FOR HALF AN HOUR, MARILYN.
OKAY. BYE!

KID-KIT?

GO-BLIT?

DER. BLUM SNIDER.

BOBA NOOP.
RALLA PEM.

THE LEAST YOU COULD DO IS SPEAK ENGLISH.
hee hee hee hee

OKAY, LET'S PLAY HIDE-AND-SEEK.
WELL... ALL RIGHT.

WE'LL HIDE, YOU SEEK!
COVER YOUR EYES AND COUNT TO ONE HUNDRED!

ONE, TWO, THREE...
IN-BRO DUGGAN, TOSH?
TOSH.
...NINETY-SEVEN, NINETY-EIGHT, NINETY-NINE...
ONE HUNDRED! READY OR NOT, HERE I COME!

FOUND
YOU!

YOU MUST KNOW ALL
THE GOOD HIDING PLACES.
WHERE SHOULD WE LOOK?
I DON'T WANT
TO LOOK.

YOU'RE THE
SEEKER. YOU
LOOK.

GROWL

UH, CAN I HAVE A
SNACK? WE DIDN'T HAVE
ONE AFTER SCHOOL.
SURE.

ALL RIGHT. YOU STAY HERE. I'LL BE BACK WHEN I FIND YOUR SISTER.
OKAY.

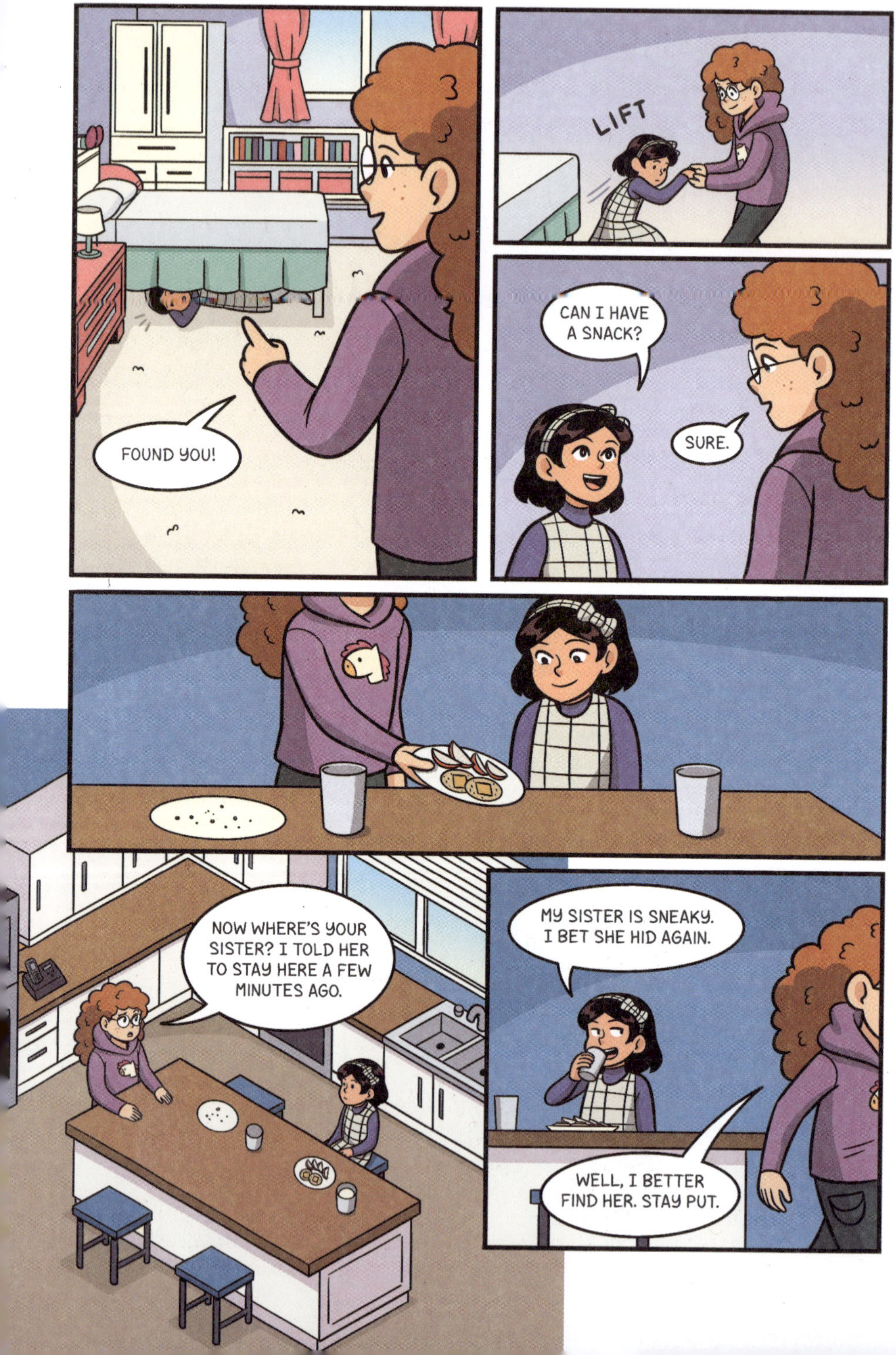

FOUND YOU!

LIFT

CAN I HAVE A SNACK?

SURE.

I LOOKED AROUND AND FINALLY FOUND A TWIN SQUISHED BEHIND A COUCH IN THE LIVING ROOM.
TOOK YOU LONG ENOUGH.
CAN I HAVE A SNACK?
YOU ALREADY HAD ONE.
NO, I DIDN'T.
WELL, I GAVE OUT TWO SNACKS.
THEN YOU GAVE BOTH OF THEM TO MY SISTER.
SORRY. IF I KNEW WHICH OF YOU WAS WHICH, THAT WOULDN'T HAVE HAPPENED.

FINE.
I'M CAROLYN. NOW CAN I HAVE MY SNACK?
I ALMOST GAVE IN, BUT MAYBE THIS TWIN ALREADY HAD TWO SNACKS AND WANTED A THIRD. MAYBE THEY NEEDED TO KNOW WHO WAS BOSS.
NOPE. NO SNACK. THERE ARE TWO OF YOU AND I GAVE OUT TWO SNACKS.
NO FAIR!
IT'S VERY FAIR.
GUMMY GROG!

WHAT?
COLLEY-MOSS. DER BLUM TIDING POFFER-TOT!
HANKY? NO GIBBLE DANDY.
GLARE
SHIVER
I WAS SORRY I MADE THEM ANGRY, BUT TOO BAD. THEY HAD TRICKED ME AGAIN.
FOR THE REST OF THE DAY, THE TWINS IGNORED ME AND CHATTED AWAY IN THEIR TWIN TALK.

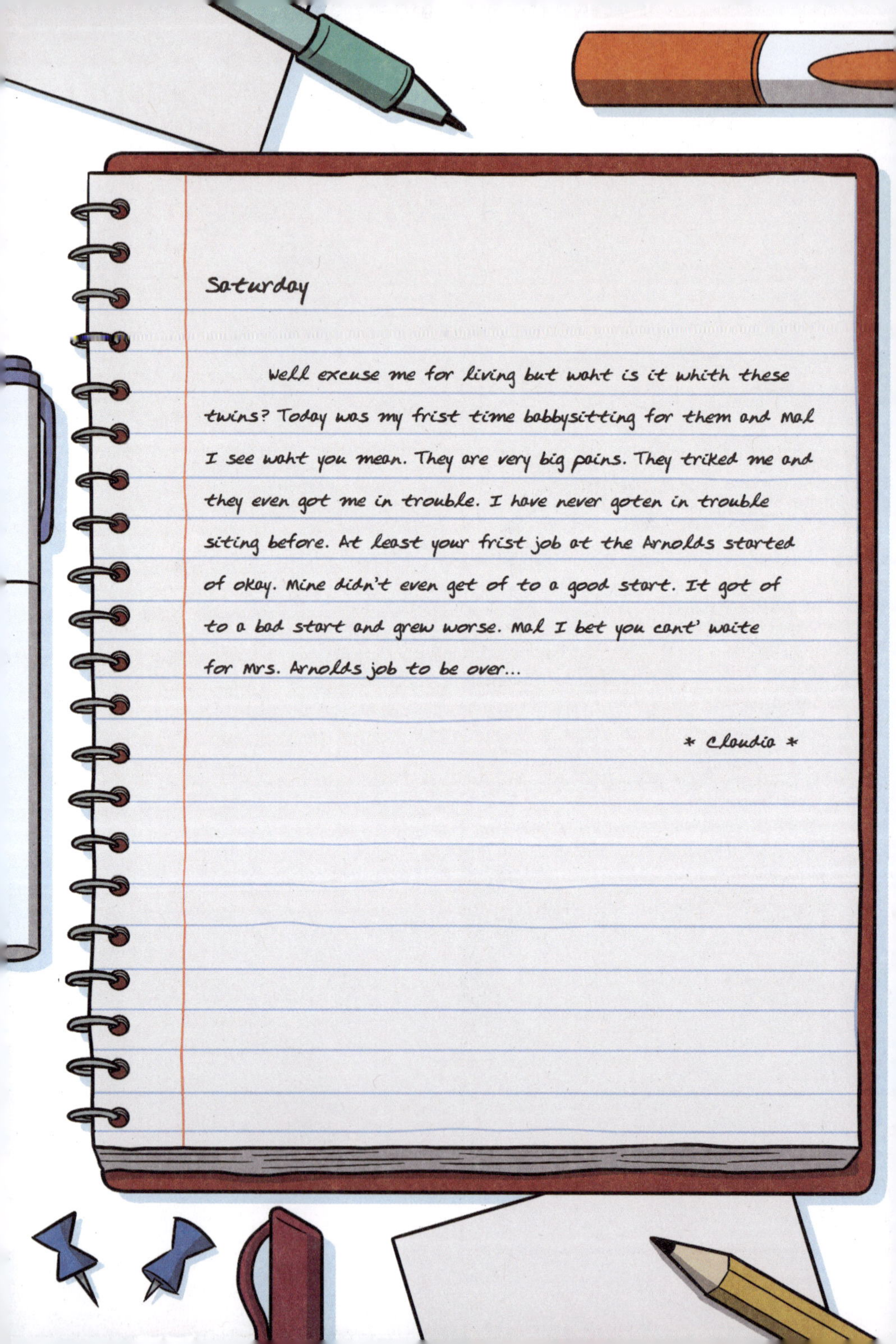

Saturday

Well excuse me for living but waht is it whith these twins? Today was my frist time babbysitting for them and Mal I see waht you mean. They are very big pains. They triked me and they even got me in trouble. I have never goten in trouble siting before. At least your frist job at the Arnolds started of okay. Mine didn't even get of to a good start. It got of to a bad start and grew worse. Mal I bet you cant' waite for Mrs. Arnolds job to be over...

* Claudia *

CHAPTER 6

CLAUDIA WAS BABY-SITTING FOR THE TWINS FROM 10:00 TO 3:00 WHILE THEIR PARENTS WENT TO AN ANTIQUE CAR SHOW IN STAMFORD.

MARILYN'S PIANO LESSON IS AT 11:30. HER CARPOOL WILL ARRIVE AT 11:00.

SHE'S GOING TO BE IN A RECITAL NEXT WEEK, AND TODAY IS A SPECIAL REHEARSAL.

SHE'LL BE BACK HOME AROUND 1:30.

WHILE MARILYN IS GONE, CAROLYN SHOULD WORK ON HER SCIENCE FAIR PROJECT. SHE JUST LOVES SCIENCE -- DON'T YOU, DEAR?

AT THAT MOMENT, THE TWINS DIDN'T APPEAR TO LOVE **ANYTHING.**

ALL RIGHT, THEN. WE'RE LEAVING!
SEE YOU LATER, KIDDOS.
BYE-BYE!

SNUFF BAT CRAWDING FOWSER. DER BLEM, TOSH?
TOSH.

I GUESS THIS IS THE PART WHERE YOU TAKE YOUR BRACELETS OFF AND TRY TO CONFUSE ME, RIGHT?

THAT'S RIGHT!

BUN MELP!
SHIN SHAM.

YOU TWO GO AHEAD AND PLAY. I DON'T CARE IF YOU DON'T WANT ME TO BE ABLE TO TELL YOU APART.

ANYWAY, I'LL BE ABLE TO TELL YOU APART AT 11:00.

MARILYN WILL LEAVE FOR HER PIANO LESSON AND CAROLYN WILL STAY TO WORK ON HER PROJECT.

mumble mumble
WELL, IF YOU GUYS ARE JUST GOING TO TALK TO EACH OTHER, I'M GOING TO READ.
YOU CAN LOOK AT THE KID-KIT IF YOU WANT.
11:00 AM
GOT EVERYTHING YOU NEED, MARILYN?
YUP!
HONK HONK

OH! THERE'S MR. BISCHOFF.
SEE YOU LATER!
BYE, MARILYN!
WHAT ARE YOU GOING TO DO WITH YOUR PROJECT TODAY, CAROLYN?
JUST FIX THE LETTERS ON THE DISPLAY AND THEN READ.
MY PROJECT IS ABOUT THE WORLD OF ELECTRICITY. I HAVE TO FIND OUT MORE ABOUT SOME EXPERIMENTS.
CLAUDIA FELT RELIEVED THAT SHE DIDN'T HAVE TO HELP CAROLYN WITH HER PROJECT.
WHAT CLAUDIA KNEW ABOUT ELECTRICITY COULD FIT ON THE HEAD OF A PIN.
PHEW

RING

HELLO,
ARNOLD
RESIDENCE.

YES, HELLO.
MRS. ARNOLD?
NO, I'M AFRAID
MRS. ARNOLD CAN'T
COME TO THE PHONE.
THIS IS CLAUDIA KISHI.
MAY I HELP YOU?
WELL...
PERHAPS.

I'M MARGARET COHEN. I TEACH PIANO AT THE MUSIC SCHOOL. I'VE GOT A VERY TONE-DEAF ARNOLD TWIN HERE, SO I'M WONDERING WHERE MARILYN IS.

YOU MEAN **CAROLYN** IS THERE?
...YES.

AUGH! THE GIRLS SWITCHED! I DON'T BELIEVE IT!

IS THERE A WAY TO, UM, SWITCH THEM BACK? MR. BISCHOFF LEFT ALREADY. I REALLY NEED TO WORK WITH MARILYN TODAY.
NO. I...I CAN'T DRIVE YET.

I'M SORRY. I GUESS CAROLYN WILL HAVE TO STAY THERE UNTIL 1:00. DO YOU MIND KEEPING HER?
UH, NO. SURE. IT'S FINE.

SIGH...

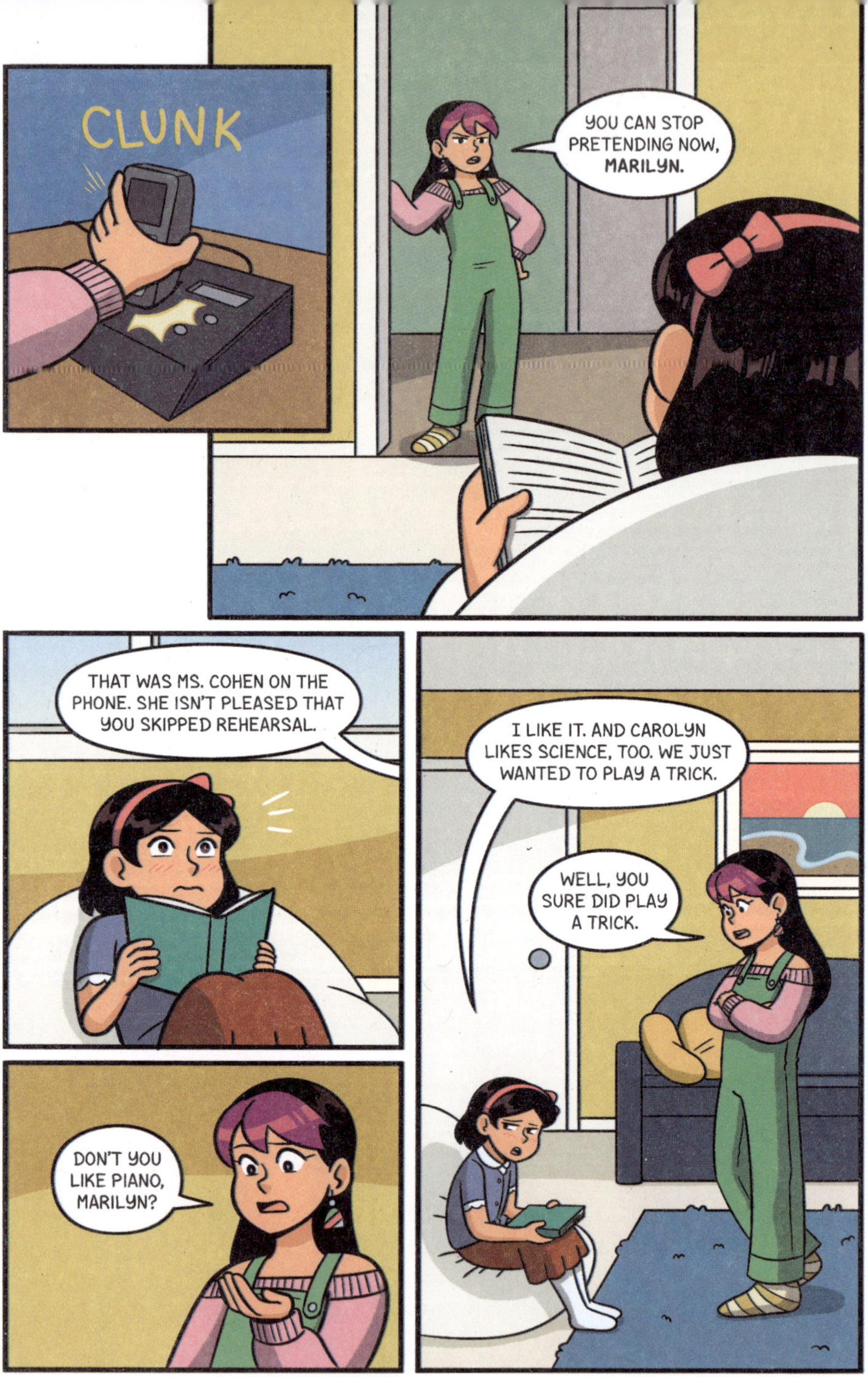

CLUNK

YOU CAN STOP PRETENDING NOW, **MARILYN.**

MS. COHEN IS UPSET, YOU'RE MISSING AN IMPORTANT REHEARSAL, AND CAROLYN IS WASTING TIME SHE COULD BE SPENDING ON THE WORLD OF ELECTRICITY.
I THINK YOU GOT YOURSELVES INTO TROUBLE.
LATER...
I'M DISAPPOINTED IN BOTH OF YOU.
WE KNOW IT MUST BE TEMPTING TO PLAY TRICKS AND JOKES, BUT YOU HAVE TO CHOOSE THE RIGHT TIMES FOR THEM.
A DAY WHEN MARILYN HAS AN IMPORTANT REHEARSAL AND CAROLYN NEEDS TO WORK ON HER SCIENCE PROJECT IS NOT A GOOD TIME.

AND, CLAUDIA, I MUST ADMIT I'M A BIT SURPRISED AT YOU.
WE UNDERSTAND THAT IT'S DIFFICULT TO TELL THEM APART WHEN THEIR BRACELETS ARE OFF.
STILL, YOU WERE RESPONSIBLE FOR THEM WHILE WE WERE OUT.
WE TRUSTED YOU TO BE IN CHARGE OF OUR DAUGHTERS.
I KNOW. I'M VERY SORRY.
THIS WAS SO UNFAIR!
I'LL UNDERSTAND IF YOU DON'T WANT ME OR ANYONE FROM OUR CLUB TO SIT FOR YOU AGAIN.
OH, NO, NO. NOTHING LIKE THAT WILL BE NECESSARY.

UNTIL CLAUDIA SAT FOR THE TWINS, I'D BEEN WORRIED THAT I WASN'T A VERY GOOD SITTER.
BUT WHEN CLAUDIA HAD TROUBLE, TOO, I REALIZED THAT THE GIRLS SIMPLY **WERE** THE TROUBLE AND NOT US BABY-SITTERS.

CHAPTER 7

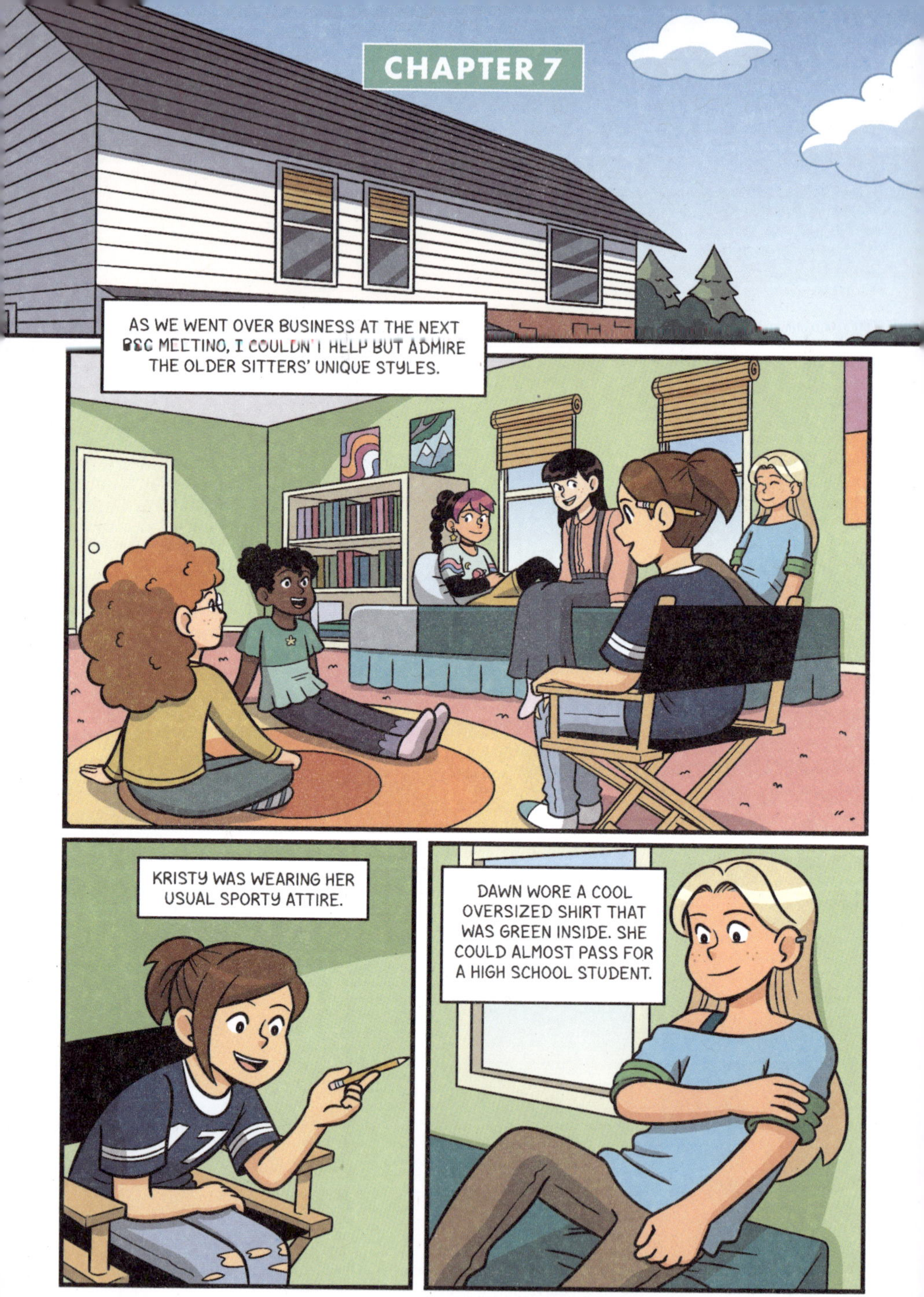

AS WE WENT OVER BUSINESS AT THE NEXT BSC MEETING, I COULDN'T HELP BUT ADMIRE THE OLDER SITTERS' UNIQUE STYLES.

MARY ANNE'S OUTFIT WAS BOTH CUTE AND MATURE. I MADE A MENTAL NOTE TO BUY MY OWN PAIR OF SUSPENDERS ONE DAY.

AND CLAUDIA HAD MADE HER EARRINGS AND PAINTED HER SHIRT HERSELF. SHE AMAZED ME.

I COULDN'T WAIT FOR THE JOB WITH THE ARNOLDS TO BE OVER. I'D HAVE ENOUGH MONEY TO BUY NEW CLOTHES AND FIGURE OUT MY OWN STYLE, TOO.

ALL RIGHT. ANY PROBLEMS? ANYTHING WE NEED TO DISCUSS?
UM, YES.
17

THE ARNOLD TWINS ARE A MAJOR PROBLEM.

I'LL SAY. THAT JOB ON SATURDAY WAS TERRIBLE.

NO PARENT HAS EVER SCOLDED ME IN FRONT OF THE KIDS I'D JUST SAT FOR. THE GIRLS MADE A BIG MESS OF THINGS. AND **WHY?** THAT'S WHAT I CAN'T FIGURE OUT.
ME NEITHER.

NO OFFENSE, MAL, BUT I HAVE TO ADMIT THAT I WENT TO THAT JOB THINKING THAT MAYBE THERE WAS SOME SORT OF PROBLEM WITH YOU AND THE ARNOLDS.

YOU KNOW, THAT THEY WERE OKAY KIDS, BUT THE THREE OF YOU JUST WEREN'T HITTING IT OFF.

IN OTHER WORDS, THAT, UM, **YOU** WERE THE PROBLEM.

DON'T WORRY ABOUT IT. I WAS WONDERING THE SAME THING MYSELF UNTIL YOU SAT FOR THEM. WE HAVE PROBLEM CLIENTS.

TO QUOTE MOM...
"I'M AT MY WITS' END."
I JUST DON'T KNOW WHAT TO DO ABOUT THE TWINS.
MAL, WE'VE READ YOUR NOTEBOOK ENTRIES, SO WE HAVE A PRETTY GOOD IDEA OF WHAT'S GOING ON, BUT TELL US AGAIN ANYWAY.
MAYBE YOU'LL THINK OF THINGS YOU DIDN'T MENTION IN THE NOTEBOOK.
OKAY.
I HAD THE COMPLETE ATTENTION OF EVERYONE IN THE ROOM, WHICH MADE ME SLIGHTLY NERVOUS.
I WANTED TO SOUND ARTICULATE AND NOT LIKE A BIG BABY. NOT LIKE SOMEONE WHO'D RUN UP AGAINST AN ANNOYING PROBLEM SHE DIDN'T FEEL LIKE HANDLING.

UM, THE TWINS **SEEM** LIKE NICE GIRLS.

THEY'RE ALWAYS BEAUTIFULLY DRESSED AND THEIR MOTHER IS, TOO.

MARILYN IS AN EXCELLENT PIANO PLAYER. SHE'S BEEN TAKING LESSONS SINCE SHE WAS FOUR.
AND CAROLYN LOVES SCIENCE.

I THINK THEY'RE SMART. THEY MUST BE SMART TO HAVE THEIR OWN TWIN TALK.

TWIN TALK?

YEAH. THEY CAN JUST BABBLE AWAY IN IT.
THINK OF HOW HARD IT IS TO LEARN A DIFFERENT LANGUAGE, LIKE FRENCH OR SPANISH.
AND THEN THINK ABOUT HOW DIFFICULT IT MUST BE TO **INVENT** A LANGUAGE.

I'M NOT SURE THE TWIN TALK IS A REAL LANGUAGE.

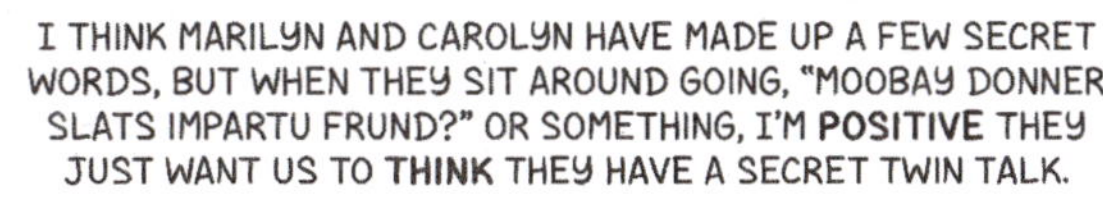
I THINK MARILYN AND CAROLYN HAVE MADE UP A FEW SECRET WORDS, BUT WHEN THEY SIT AROUND GOING, "MOOBAY DONNER SLATS IMPARTU FRUND?" OR SOMETHING, I'M **POSITIVE** THEY JUST WANT US TO **THINK** THEY HAVE A SECRET TWIN TALK.

BUT WHY DO THEY DO THAT? AND WHY DO THEY TAKE OFF THEIR BRACELETS AND CONFUSE ME?

THEY'RE MEAN, AND I WAS NEVER MEAN TO THEM.

MAYBE THOSE ARE JUST THINGS IDENTICAL TWINS DO?

I DONT KNOW. THE TRIPLETS ARE IDENTICAL AND THEY DON'T DO STUFF LIKE THAT.
NOT EVEN TO PEOPLE WHO CAN'T TELL THEM APART.

I MEAN, SURE, THEY'VE PLAYED A FEW TRICKS, LIKE SWITCHING PLACES IN SCHOOL WHEN THERE WAS A SUBSTITUTE TEACHER.

BUT ALL KIDS TRY TO TRICK SUBSTITUTES. IT'S, LIKE, A **LAW**.
ha ha
ha ha
ha ha

YOU KNOW, I DON'T THINK THERE'S MUCH YOU CAN DO ABOUT THE TWINS.
IT SOUNDS LIKE YOU'RE BEING THE BEST BABY-SITTER YOU CAN BE, AND THEY'RE JUST BRATS.
17

YOU'LL HAVE TO FINISH YOUR JOB WITH THEM, BUT AFTER THAT, I WON'T EXPECT ANYONE TO FEEL THEY HAVE TO TAKE A JOB AT THE ARNOLDS'.

IF MRS. ARNOLD CALLS AGAIN, WE'LL JUST TELL HER WE'RE BUSY. I DON'T LIKE DOING THAT, BUT I THINK WE'LL HAVE TO.
17

BOY... IT'S TOO BAD. THEY'RE REALLY CUTE KIDS.

I BET YOU CAN'T WAIT FOR YOUR LAST DAY WITH THE ARNOLDS.
OH, YEAH, DEFINITELY.
IT'LL BE GREAT! I'LL BE DONE WITH THE TROUBLESOME TWINS **AND** I'LL GET MY EARS PIERCED AND A DECENT HAIRCUT.
I WANT PIERCED EARS AND A DECENT HAIRCUT, TOO.
I WANT ONE MORE HOLE IN MY RIGHT EAR.
AND I WANT TO GET BACK TO BUSINESS.
PART OF ME WAS DISAPPOINTED. I HADN'T GOTTEN ANY SUGGESTIONS ON HOW TO WORK WITH THE TWINS -- AND I WOULD HAVE TO FACE THEM AGAIN THE VERY NEXT AFTERNOON.

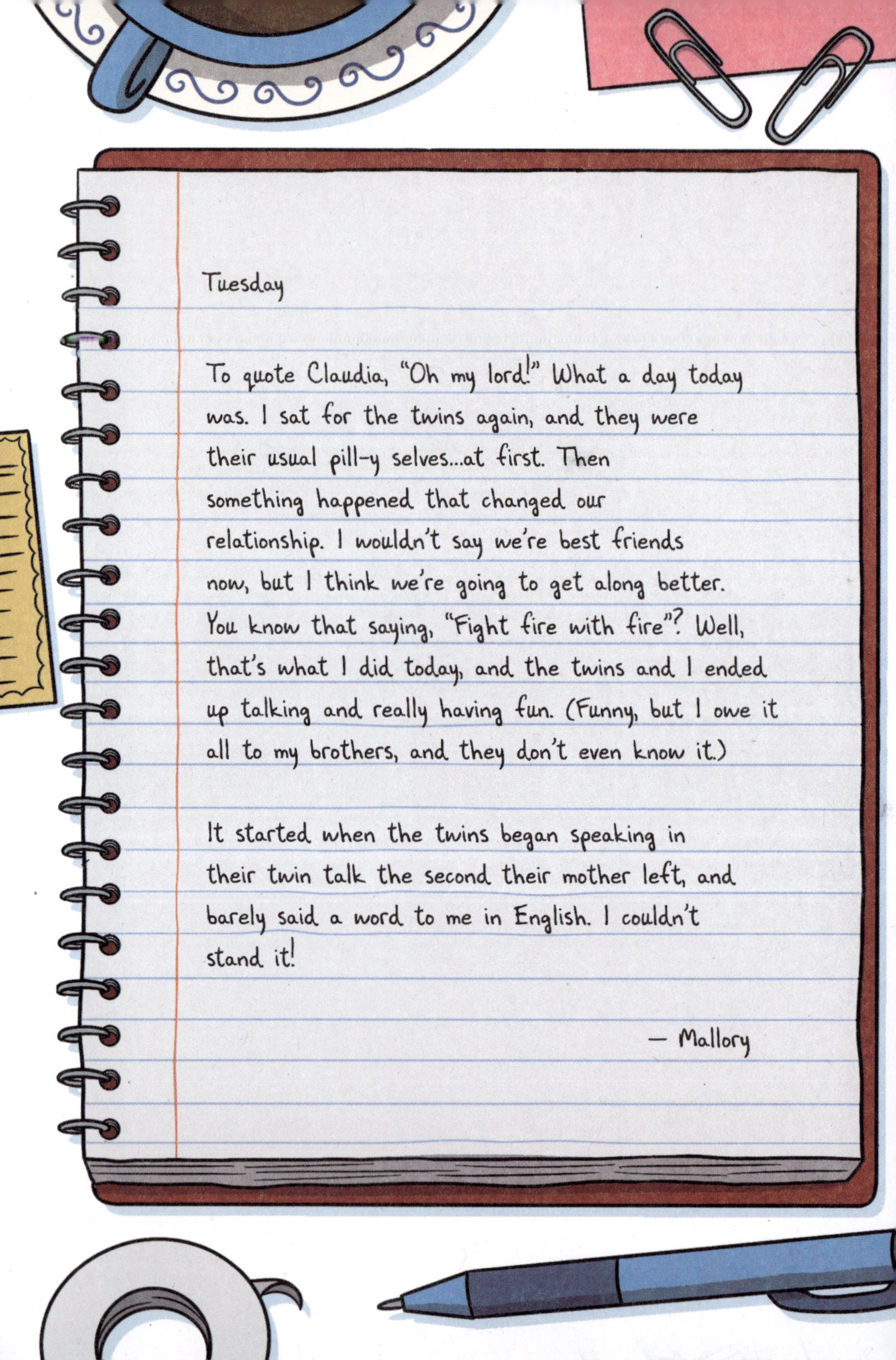
Tuesday
To quote Claudia, "Oh my lord!" What a day today was. I sat for the twins again, and they were their usual pill-y selves...at first. Then something happened that changed our relationship. I wouldn't say we're best friends now, but I think we're going to get along better. You know that saying, "Fight fire with fire"? Well, that's what I did today, and the twins and I ended up talking and really having fun. (Funny, but I owe it all to my brothers, and they don't even know it.)
It started when the twins began speaking in their twin talk the second their mother left, and barely said a word to me in English. I couldn't stand it!
— Mallory

CHAPTER 8

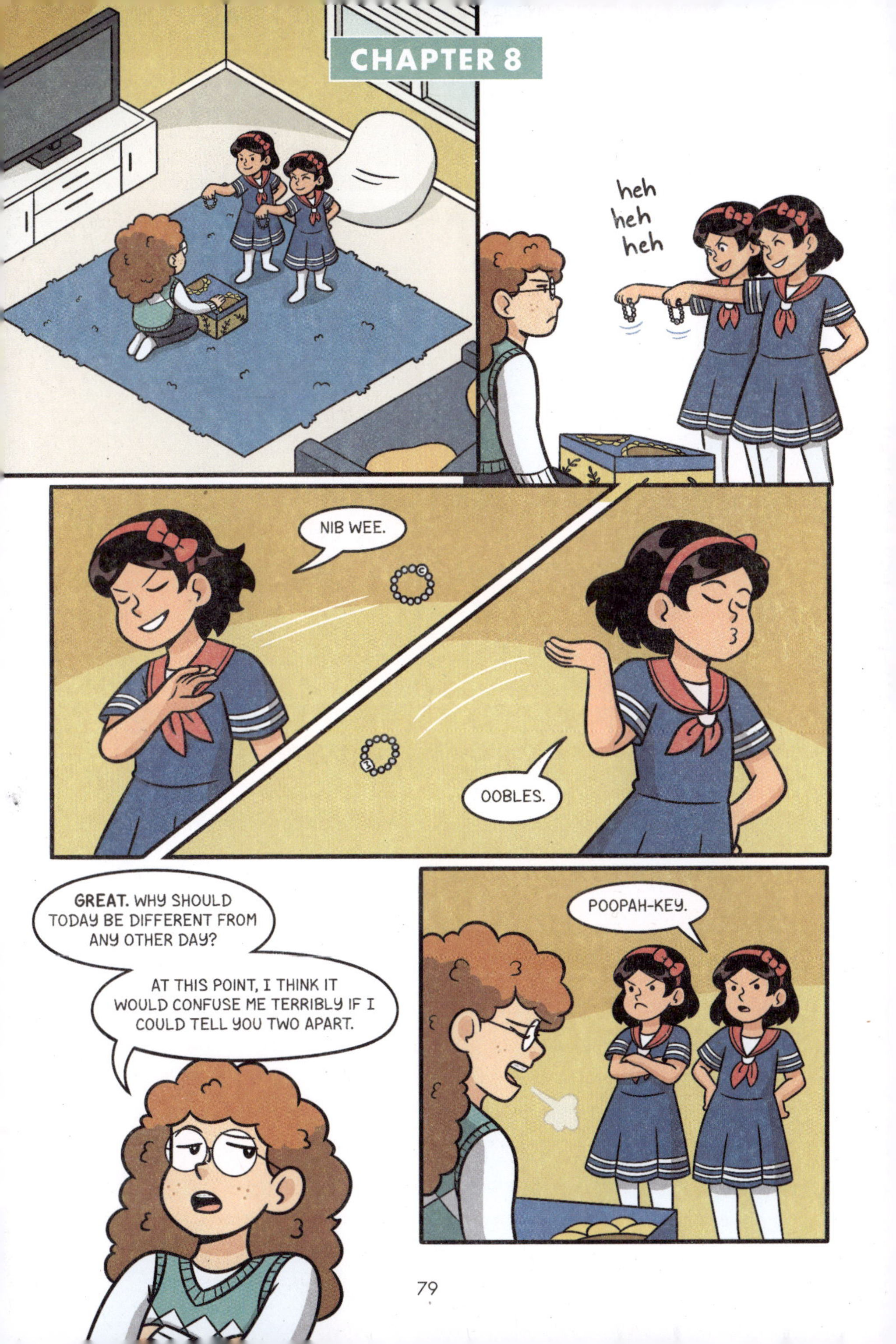

heh
heh
heh

NIB WEE.

OOBLES.

LOOK, HERE'S A STICKER BOOK.
AND I BROUGHT CAROLYN A BOOK ABOUT ELECTRICITY. I BORROWED IT FROM MY BROTHER ADAM.
1000 ADORABLE PUPPY STICKERS

HMM. TIBBLE VAN CARMIN.

HOW ABOUT PUZZLES?

ZOO MAT.

CHUTES AND LADDERS?
PERRING DU SUMMERFLAT.

OKAY, GO AHEAD. HAVE FUN.
PUSH

TEN MINUTES LATER

MALLORY.

CAN I HAVE AN ICE CREAM SANDWICH? WE HAVE A BOX OF THEM IN OUR FREEZER.

OUT OF THE BLUE, I HAD AN IDEA.

I COULD GIVE THE TWINS A TASTE OF THEIR OWN MEDICINE. FIGHT FIRE WITH FIRE.

AT'S-THAY INE-FAY ITH-WAY EE-MAY.

WHAT?

WHAT ARE YOU SAYING?

I'M-HAY AYING-SAY AT-THAY OO-YAY AN-CAY AVE-HAY A-HAY ACK-SNAY. O-SAY AN-CAY OUR-YAY ISTER-SAY.

TALK TO US!
I-HAY AM-HAY ALKING-TAY OO-TAY OO-YAY.

TALK IN ENGLISH! STOP TALKING LIKE THAT!

YOU TWO HAVEN'T BEEN SPEAKING TO **ME** IN ENGLISH.
MALVERN TOPPIT SAMWAÝ.

UT'S-WHAY IS-THAY? ORE-MAY IN-TWAY ALK-TAY?
UGHH!

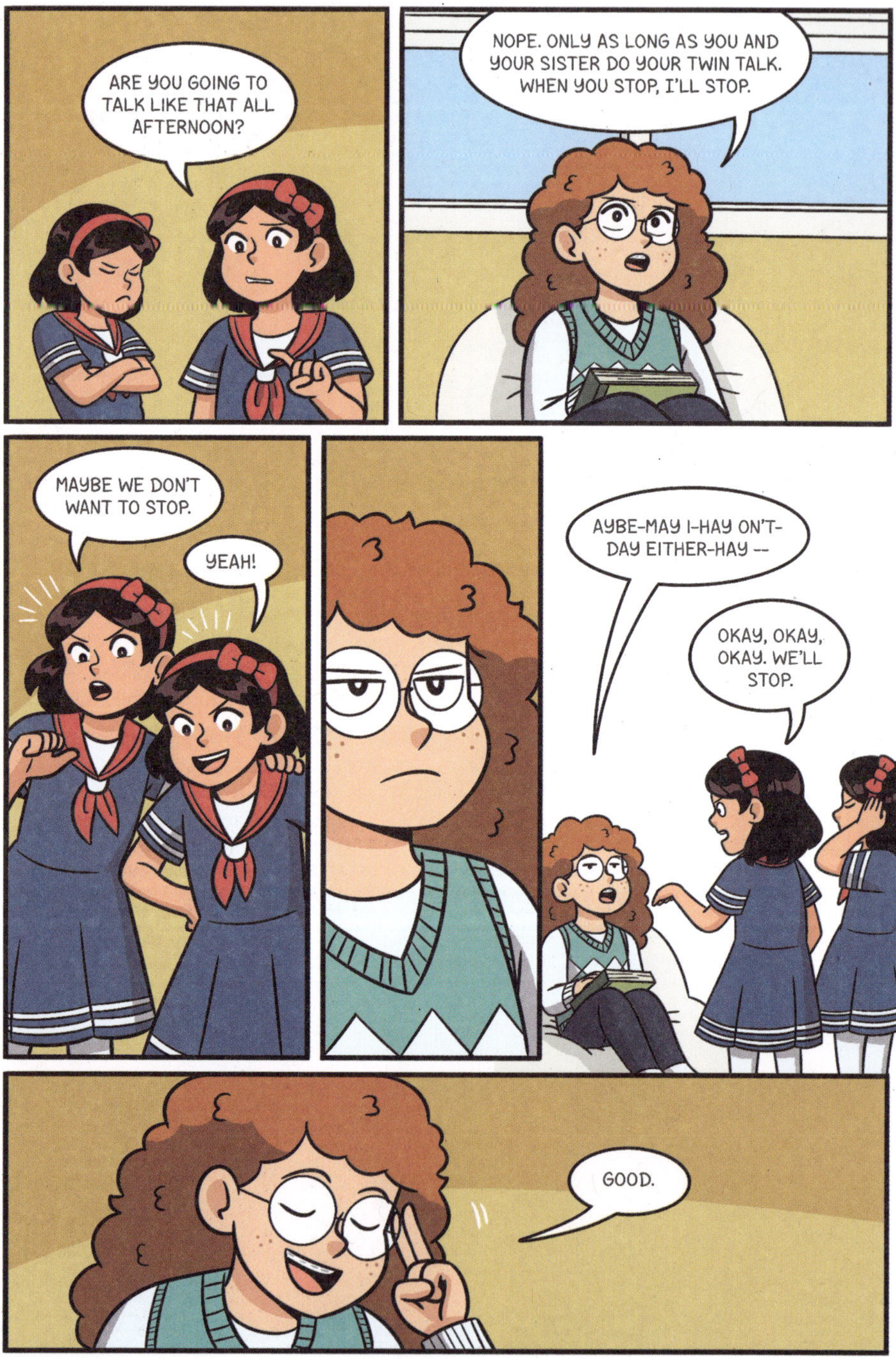

ARE YOU GOING TO TALK LIKE THAT ALL AFTERNOON?

MAYBE WE DON'T WANT TO STOP.

YEAH!

AYBE-MAY I-HAY ON'T-DAY EITHER-HAY --

OKAY, OKAY, OKAY. WE'LL STOP.

NOW YOU KNOW HOW IT FEELS WHEN YOU LEAVE SOMEONE OUT OF THE CONVERSATION. OR WHEN YOU'RE RUDE TO THEM.

WHAT LANGUAGE WERE YOU TALKING IN?

PIG LATIN.
PIG LATIN?

YUP. MY BROTHERS TAUGHT IT TO ME. THEY TALK IN IT SOMETIMES WHEN THEY NEED A PRIVATE LANGUAGE.

I COULD TEACH IT TO YOU...

BUT YOU'VE GOT A LANGUAGE OF YOUR OWN. YOU PROBABLY DON'T NEED PIG LATIN.

OH YES!
YES, WE DO!
TEACH US!!
OKAY,
OKAY.

I'LL TEACH YOU ON
TWO CONDITIONS.

ONE, THAT YOU PUT
YOUR BRACELETS ON --
AND ON **RIGHT.**

I'LL JUST HAVE TO TRUST
THAT YOU DO IT RIGHT. BUT I
REALLY WANT TO BE ABLE
TO TELL YOU APART.

AND TWO, THAT
AFTER I TEACH YOU PIG
LATIN, YOU STOP USING
YOUR OWN LANGUAGE
AROUND ME. IS
THAT A DEAL?

whisper
whisper

IF YOU ASK FOR TWO THINGS, THEN WE WANT TWO THINGS, TOO.
ALL RIGHT.

WE WANT TO LEARN PIG LATIN, AND WE WANT ICE CREAM SANDWICHES.
NOD

FAIR ENOUGH.
YAY!

MALLORY, DO YOU REALLY WANT TO BE ABLE TO TELL US APART?
WE'RE SO TIRED OF LOOKING ALIKE.
YES. I REALLY DO.
THERE MUST BE **SOME** DIFFERENCE BETWEEN YOU. SOMETHING BESIDES THE BRACELETS.
WELL...THERE IS ONE THING.
ARE YOU REALLY GOING TO TELL HER?
IT'S ALL RIGHT. SHE SAID SHE WANTS TO KNOW.
IT'LL BE FINE. OKAY?
OKAY.
LOOK VERY CLOSELY AT OUR FACES.
LOOK AT OUR CHEEKS.

HMM...

THE MOLES! CAROLYN HAS ONE ON HER LEFT CHEEK AND MARILYN HAS ONE ON HER RIGHT!
NOD
IT'S THE ONLY DIFFERENCE BETWEEN US THAT'S EASY TO SEE.

THANK YOU FOR TELLING ME.

NOW I'LL KEEP MY PART OF THE BARGAIN AND TEACH YOU PIG LATIN.
YES!

TAKE THE SOUND AT THE BEGINNING OF A WORD, DROP IT, SAY THE REST OF THE WORD, AND FOLLOW IT UP WITH THAT SOUND PLUS "AY." TRY IT WITH YOUR NAMES.
ARILYN-MAY!
AROLYN-CAY!

THE REST OF THE AFTERNOON WAS A DREAM. THEY DIDN'T PLAY ANY TRICKS ON ME.

WHEN MRS. ARNOLD CAME HOME, SHE ASKED ME THE LAST QUESTION I WOULD'VE EXPECTED TO HEAR AFTER WHAT HAPPENED WITH CLAUDIA.
THE TWINS' EIGHTH BIRTHDAY IS COMING UP AND THEY'RE GOING TO HAVE A BIG PARTY.
WOULD YOU AND TWO OF YOUR FRIENDS WANT TO COME HELP?

I'LL TELL THE GIRLS ABOUT IT AT OUR MEETING TOMORROW, AND THEN I'LL CALL TO LET YOU KNOW IF WE CAN DO IT.
SOUNDS GOOD!

OOD-GAY EYE-BAY!
EYE-BAY!

Sunday

Today was pretty interesting. I thought it was going to be just another afternoon sitting job at my house, but I guess by now I should know better. There isn't any such thing as just another sitting job - not with Karen, Andrew, and David Michael. Oh, nothing bad happened, but something surprising did. You never know what to expect from little kids. I guess the important thing to remember is that a kid is not just a kid. A kid is a person - a human being - who happens to be shorter and younger than an adult.

Anyway, the afternoon started off quietly. Hannie and Linny Papadakis came over to play with Karen and David Michael, while I tried to help Andrew memorize lines for this program he's going to be in at his preschool...

- Kristy

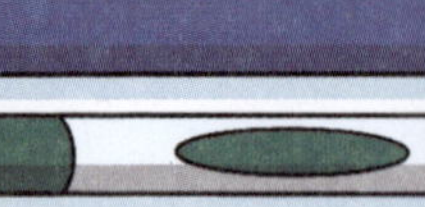

CHAPTER 9

ALL RIGHT. LET'S SEE. JASON THE RINGMASTER SAYS, "AND NOW, ALL THE WAY FROM EUROPE, HERE IS THE FAMOUS SKATING BEAR!"
RIGHT. AND I'M PLAYING THE BEAR. I'M SUPPOSED TO SAY...

"I AM...I AM" UMM...

KRISTY, I FORGET WHAT I'M SUPPOSED TO SAY, AND ANYWAY, I DON'T WANT TO SAY IT.
I DON'T WANT TO STAND UP AND TALK AT **ALL**.
I KNOW YOU DON'T, BUT YOU HAVE TO. THAT'S YOUR JOB.

YOU KNOW HOW YOUR DADDY AND MOMMY HAVE JOBS AND GO TO WORK?
YEAH.

AND MY MOTHER AND YOUR STEPFATHER HAVE JOBS AND GO TO WORK?
YEAH.

WELL, I HAVE JOBS, TOO. MY JOBS ARE BABY-SITTING AND GOING TO SCHOOL.
GOING TO SCHOOL IS ALSO A JOB FOR CHARLIE, SAM, DAVID MICHAEL, KAREN, AND YOU.
PART OF **YOUR** JOB IS TO BE IN THIS PROGRAM.

BUT I DON'T WANT TO BE IN IT. I DON'T WANT EVERYONE LOOKING AT AND LISTENING TO ME.

BUT YOU KNOW WHAT THEY'LL PROBABLY BE THINKING WHILE THEY'RE DOING THAT?
WHAT?

THEY'LL PROBABLY BE THINKING, WHAT A GOOD BEAR THAT ANDREW MAKES. HE KNOWS HIS LINES SO WELL. I BET HE WORKED VERY HARD.

WHAT IF I FORGET MY LINES? THEN WHAT WILL THEY BE THINKING?

THEY'LL BE THINKING, OH, TOO BAD. HE FORGOT HIS LINES. WELL, THAT HAPPENS SOMETIMES. HE STILL LOOKS LIKE A VERY NICE, SMART BOY.

UM, I'D LIKE TO BE ALONE FOR A BIT.
CAN I PLEASE GO TO MY ROOM?

SURE. WE CAN PRACTICE AGAIN LATER, OKAY?
OKAY.

HEY, HOW'S IT GOING?
KRISTY!
LOOK WHAT HANNIE GOT! IT'S LIKE THE MATCHING DRESSES THAT NANNIE GAVE US!
MY MOMMY BOUGHT IT FOR ME, AND AS SOON AS I SAW IT I SAID, "THAT'S JUST LIKE KAREN'S DRESS."
AFTER WE FINISHED COLORING, I CHANGED INTO IT AND SURPRISED KAREN!
ARE WE TWINS?
YOU LOOK JUST LIKE TWINS.

LET'S DO SOMETHING THAT TWINS DO!
YES!
KRISTY HAD AN IDEA OF HER OWN.
HI, YOU GUYS!

WHAT DO YOU THINK?

I --

I THINK WE'RE TIRED OF BEING TWINS.
YEAH...

I'LL CHANGE.
GOOD IDEA.

I GUESS I'LL CHANGE, TOO.

Prakash Books India Pvt Lt[illegible] Delhi

Un'Approved Worksheet

For checking purpose only

Bill To

MIDLAND THE BOOK SH[illegible] DELHI

SHOP NO. 20, AURO P[illegible]

HAUZ KHAS

NEW-DELHI - 110 016

DELHI State Code : 7

GSTIN : NA

Ser	ISBN/Code	HSN	Title
CO No : Zuber Baig - BIO - PRH			Date : 27
1	9780670096008	49011010	Bose: The Untold Story
2	9780552170536	49011010	Serve To Win
3	9780670092369	49011010	Rajneeti: A Biography
4	9781644213544	49011010	A Man'S Place

mumble mumble
"I AM..."
"I AM BENJAMIN, THE BEST ROLLER-SKATING BEAR IN THE WORLD!"

ANDREW WAS AFRAID AND SHY, BUT IF HE **HAD** TO PERFORM, HE WANTED TO DO IT WELL.
whew...

KRISTY WAS PROUD OF HIM.

ha ha
ha ha

"INTERESTING," KRISTY WROTE IN THE CLUB NOTEBOOK. "JESSI SAID GIRLS THIS AGE LIKE TO PRETEND THEY'RE TWINS, BUT KAREN SAID THEY GOT TIRED OF THE GAME."
I THOUGHT ABOUT THAT ENTRY FOR A LONG TIME.
I THOUGHT ABOUT THE THINGS MARILYN AND CAROLYN SAID TO ME.
I THOUGHT ABOUT WHAT JESSI SAID -- THAT IT'S FUN TO **PRETEND** YOU HAVE A TWIN.

THEN I THOUGHT ABOUT ME.
I REMEMBERED A TIME A YEAR AGO WHEN I HAD BOUGHT THIS VERY COOL FLOPPY BOW FOR MY HAIR.
VANESSA LIKED IT SO MUCH THAT TWO DAYS LATER, SHE BOUGHT ONE, TOO.
I WAS SO ANGRY. WHENEVER SHE WORE HER BOW TO SCHOOL, I WOULDN'T WEAR MINE.
I WANTED TO BE AN INDIVIDUAL. SOMEONE WHO INSISTED ON BEING UNIQUE. ON BEING **HERSELF**.

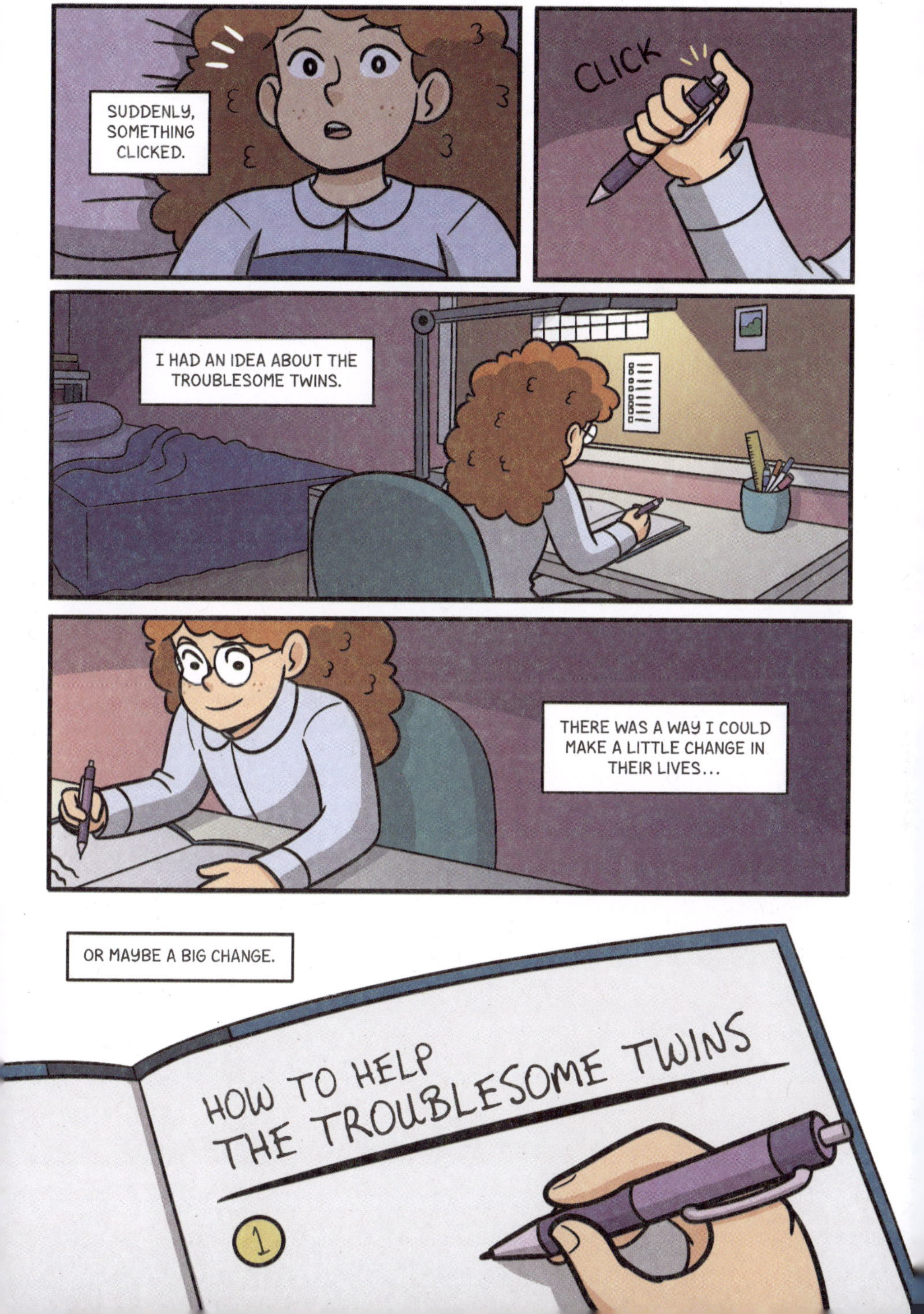

OR MAYBE A BIG CHANGE.

HOW TO HELP
THE TROUBLESOME TWINS

1

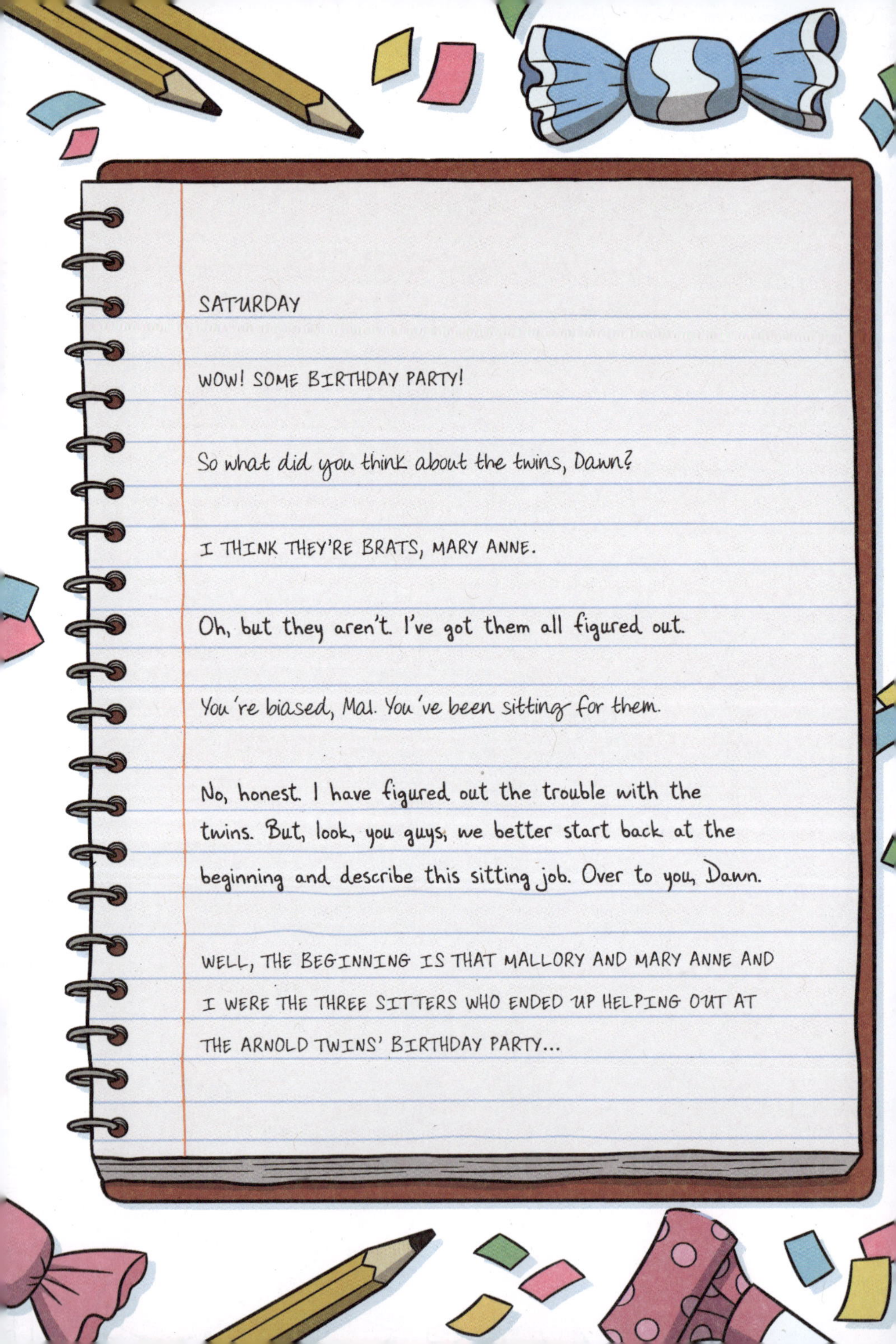
SATURDAY
WOW! SOME BIRTHDAY PARTY!
So what did you think about the twins, Dawn?
I THINK THEY'RE BRATS, MARY ANNE.
Oh, but they aren't. I've got them all figured out.
You're biased, Mal. You've been sitting for them.
No, honest. I have figured out the trouble with the twins. But, look, you guys, we better start back at the beginning and describe this sitting job. Over to you, Dawn.
WELL, THE BEGINNING IS THAT MALLORY AND MARY ANNE AND I WERE THE THREE SITTERS WHO ENDED UP HELPING OUT AT THE ARNOLD TWINS' BIRTHDAY PARTY...

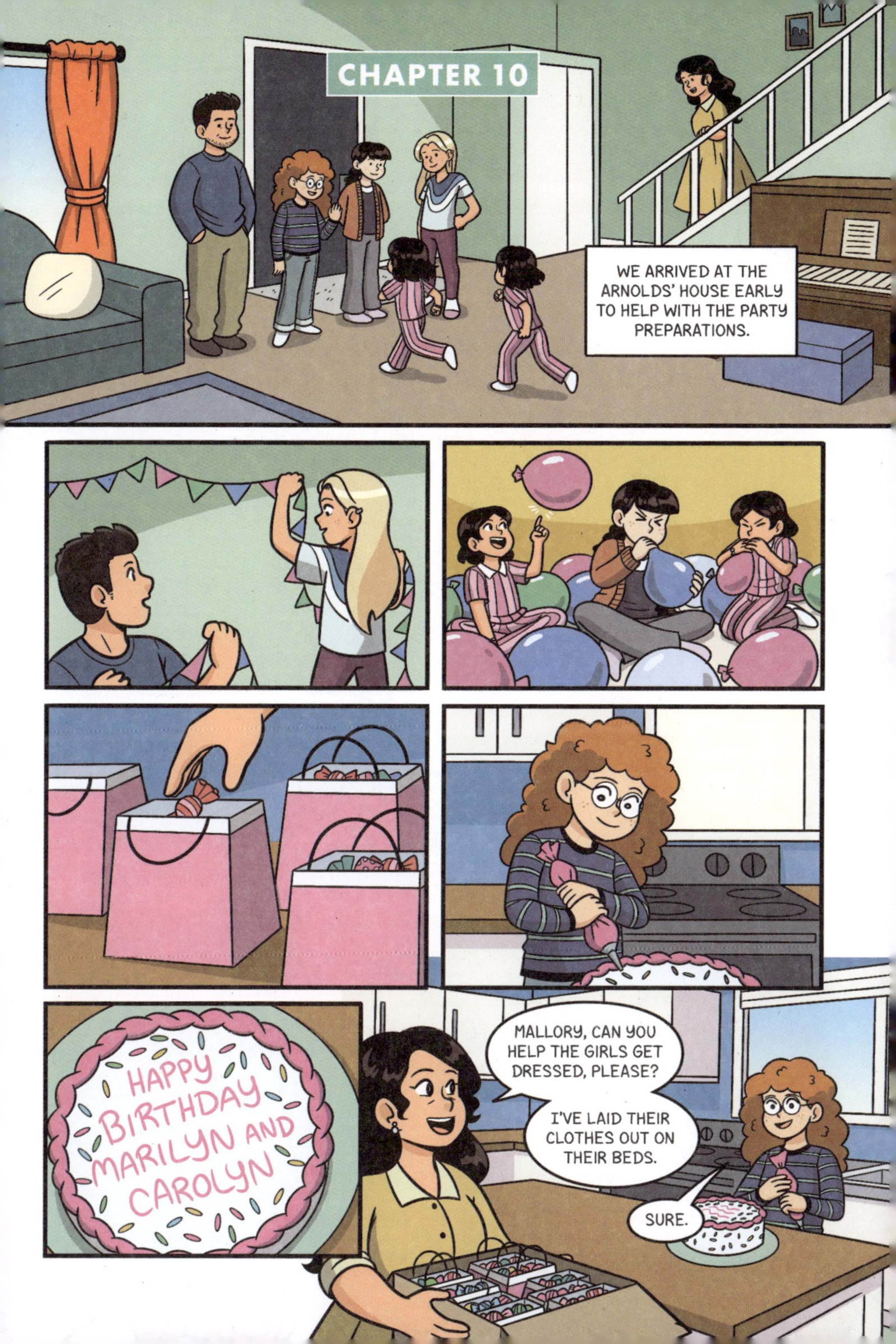

CHAPTER 10

WE ARRIVED AT THE ARNOLDS' HOUSE EARLY TO HELP WITH THE PARTY PREPARATIONS.

MALLORY, CAN YOU HELP THE GIRLS GET DRESSED, PLEASE?

I'VE LAID THEIR CLOTHES OUT ON THEIR BEDS.

SURE.

THESE ARE GORGEOUS! ARE THEY NEW?
YES.

GOSH.
YOU GUYS PROBABLY DON'T LIKE HAVING TO DRESS THE SAME ALL THE TIME. I'M NOT SURE I'D LIKE IT.
YEAH...
LAST YEAR WE **LOVED** WEARING THE SAME DRESSES.
THIS YEAR, IT JUST DOESN'T SEEM LIKE FUN ANYMORE.
HARDLY ANYONE KNOWS WHETHER I'M MARILYN OR CAROLYN. NO ONE EVEN CARES.
IT'S LIKE WE'RE ONE PERSON INSTEAD OF TWO.

MAYBE YOU COULD DRESS DIFFERENTLY TODAY.
ONE OF YOU COULD WEAR YOUR SAILOR DRESS. THAT COULD BE GOOD FOR A BIRTHDAY PARTY.
NO...WE HAVE TO WEAR WHAT MOMMY SAYS.
OH. ALL RIGHT.

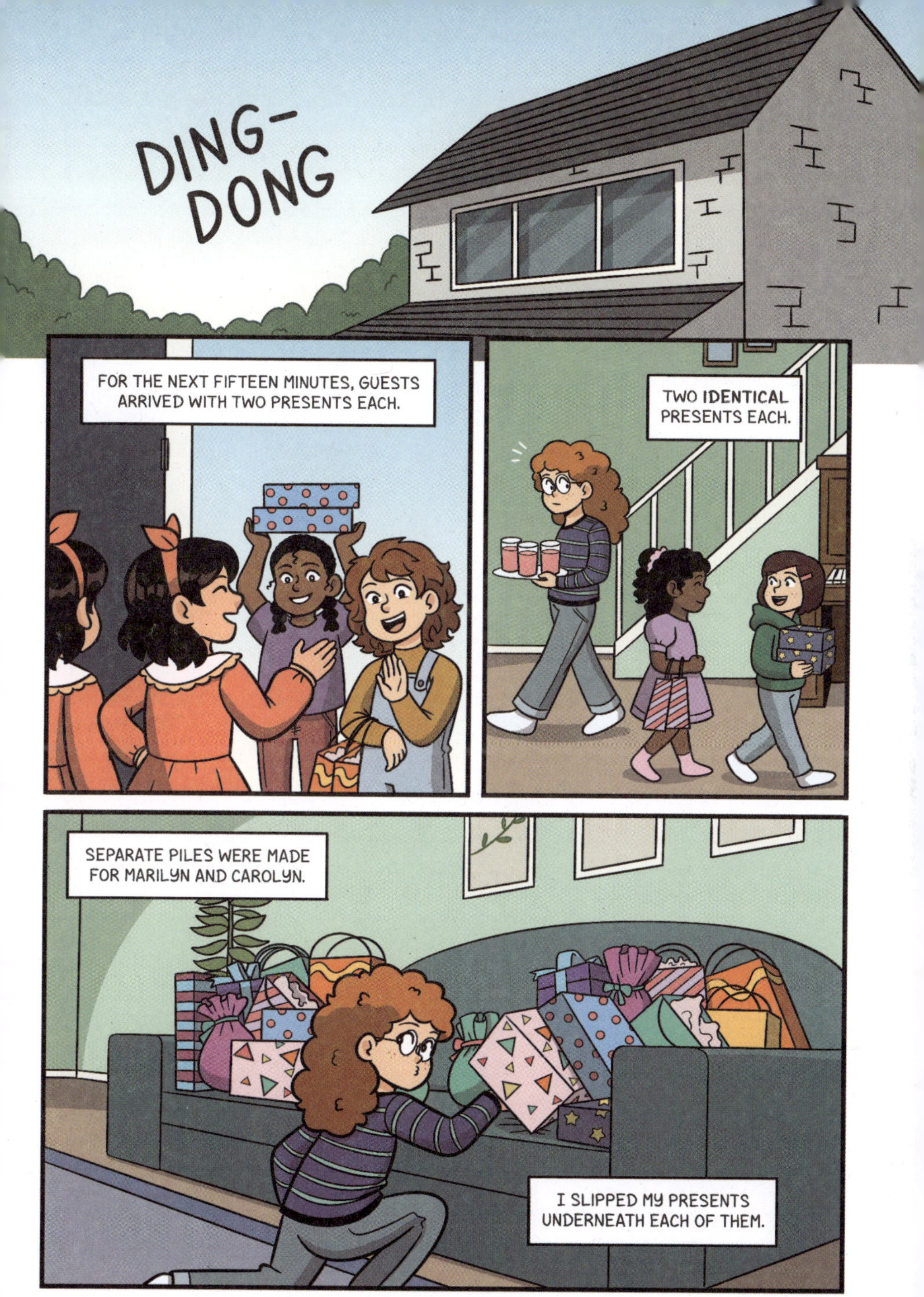

DING-
DONG

FOR THE NEXT FIFTEEN MINUTES, GUESTS ARRIVED WITH TWO PRESENTS EACH.

TWO **IDENTICAL** PRESENTS EACH.

THEN IT WAS TIME TO PARTY!

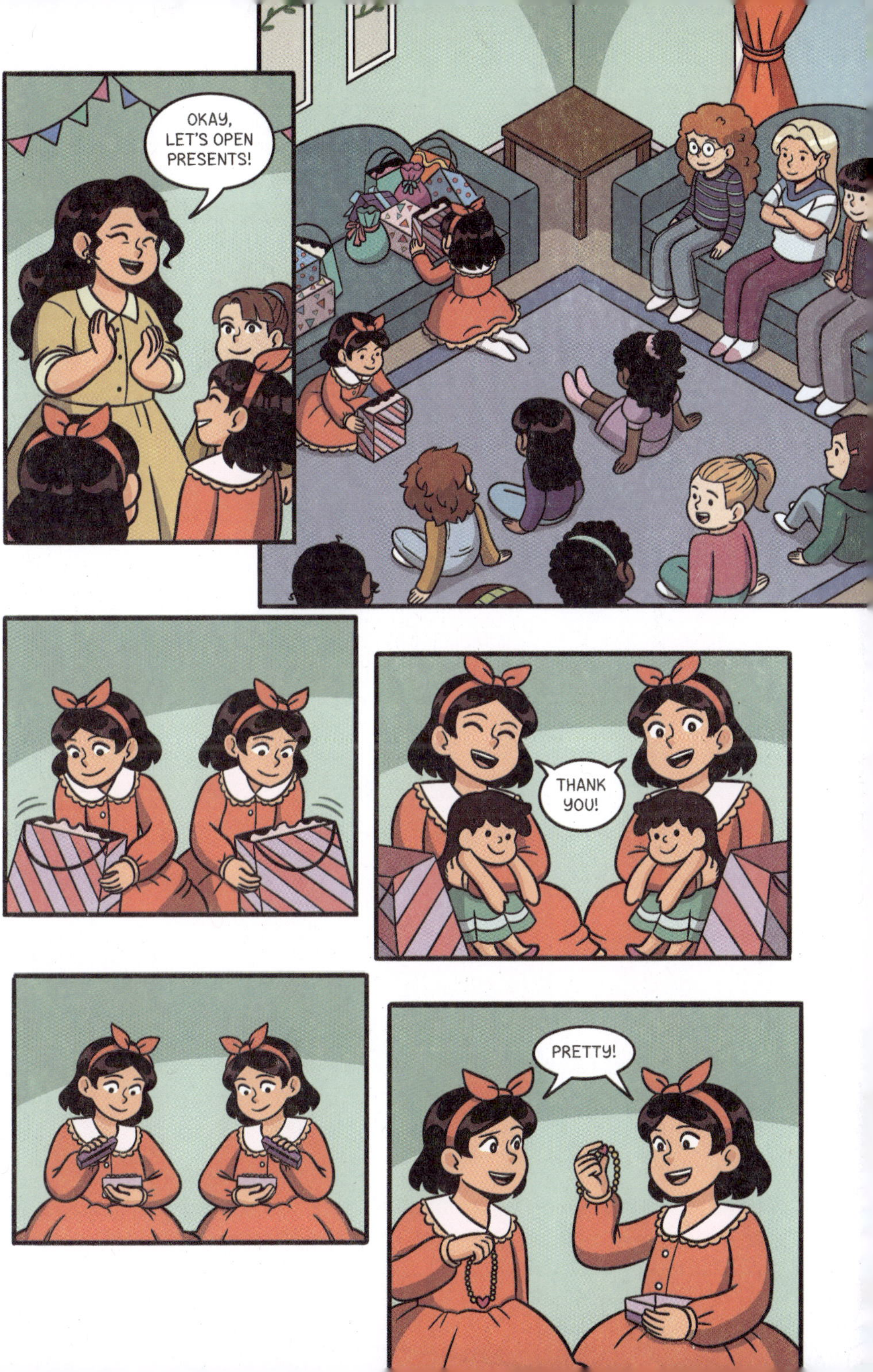

OKAY, LET'S OPEN PRESENTS!

COOL.

GREAT...

AT LAST, THE ONLY PRESENTS LEFT WERE MINE.

IS THIS A MISTAKE?

WHO ARE THEY FROM?

ME. GO AHEAD AND OPEN THEM.

rustle
rustle

IT'S A PIANO PIN!
WHOA! A BOOK ABOUT SCIENCE EXPERIMENTS!

THANK YOU, MALLORY! THANK YOU!
YOU'RE WELCOME.

AFTERWARD, MRS. ARNOLD WANTED TO TAKE SOME PICTURES.
THE GIRLS WERE ALWAYS TOGETHER, ALWAYS DOING THE SAME THINGS.
IT WAS NO WONDER THAT BY CAKE TIME, THEIR FACES WERE IDENTICAL THUNDERCLOUDS.

I FELT BAD FOR THE TWINS.
THEY WANTED TO BE INDIVIDUALS,
NOT JUST MARILYN-OR-CAROLYN,
A CUTE LOOK-ALIKE TWIN.

AND I PLANNED TO DO
SOMETHING ABOUT IT.

CHAPTER 11

THREE DAYS LATER
HI, MALLORY!
HI, GUYS.
HI! HI! HI!
OOF!
WE COULDN'T WAIT FOR YOU TO GET HERE!
COME CHECK OUT OUR NEW GIFTS.

THESE ARE FROM AUNT ELAINE AND UNCLE FRANK!

JUMP ROPES!

NEAT!

MOMMY AND DADDY GAVE US THESE.

BEDS FOR OUR DOLLS.

NICE.

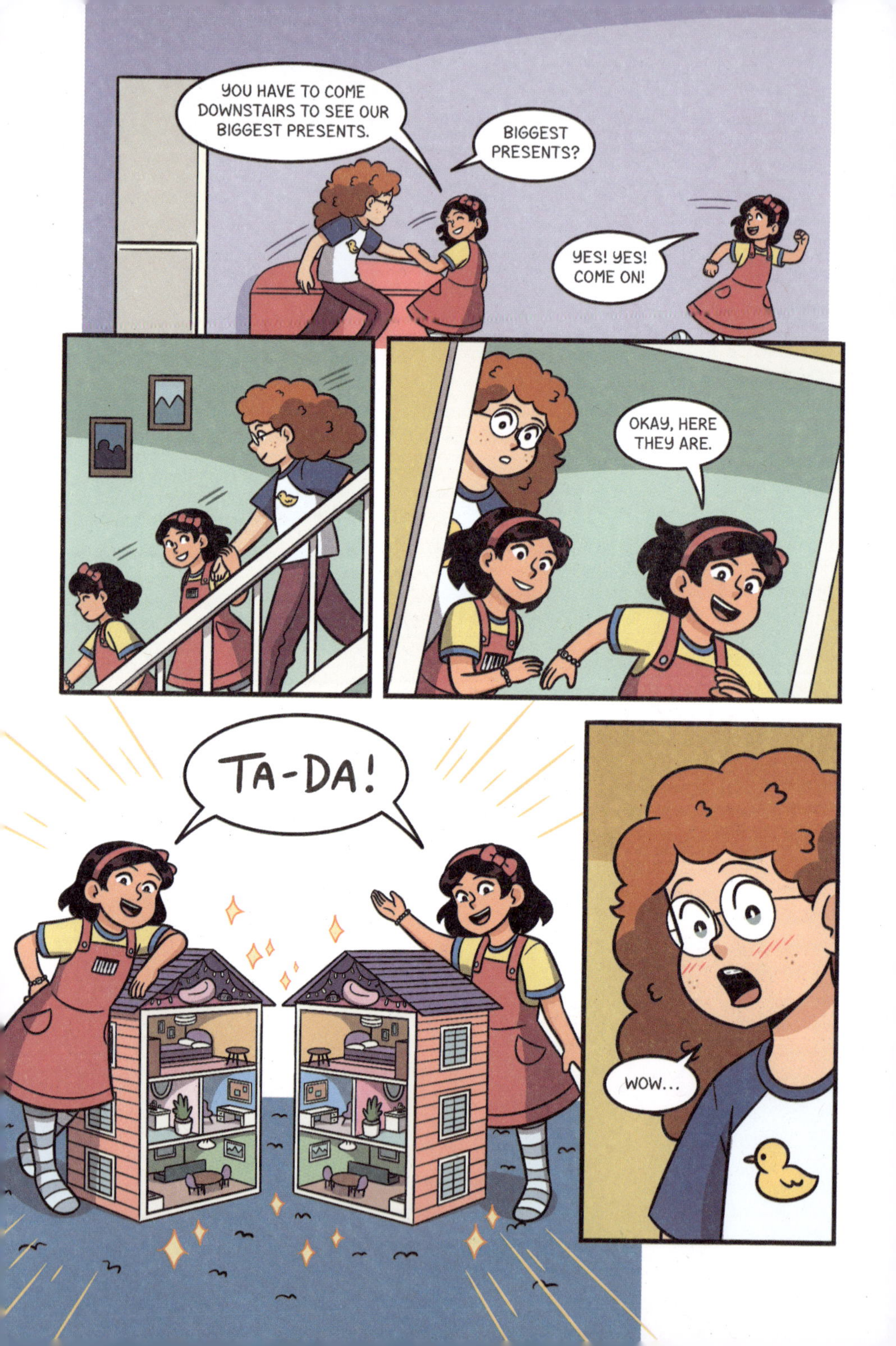

YOU HAVE TO COME DOWNSTAIRS TO SEE OUR BIGGEST PRESENTS.

BIGGEST PRESENTS?

YES! YES! COME ON!

OKAY, HERE THEY ARE.

LOOK, IF I PRESS THIS BUTTON IN THE BACK, LIGHTS TURN ON IN EACH ROOM!

AND THEY CAME WITH ALL THIS TINY FURNITURE AND PLATES OF FOOD.

THESE ARE AMAZING!!

GUESS WHAT OUR BEST PRESENTS ARE?
THE DOLLHOUSES, OF COURSE!

shake shake
NOPE.

IT'S THE PIANO PIN AND THE SCIENCE BOOK.

MY PRESENTS?! HOW COME?

BECAUSE...

THEY WERE DIFFERENT.
AND THEY WERE MEANT FOR US.

IT SEEMS LIKE YOU **REALLY** KNOW US. IS... IS THAT SILLY?

OF COURSE NOT. IT ISN'T SILLY AT ALL.

DID I EVER TELL YOU THAT THREE OF MY BROTHERS ARE TRIPLETS?
NO! THEY ARE?

YUP. AND OUR FAMILY NEVER TREATS THEM LIKE THEY'RE ALL ONE PERSON.
I THINK MAYBE THAT'S BECAUSE THERE ARE SO MANY KIDS IN OUR FAMILY.
THERE WOULDN'T BE ANY POINT IN TREATING THE THREE OF THEM LIKE ONE PERSON AND THE REST OF THE KIDS LIKE FIVE DIFFERENT PEOPLE.

SO YOUR BROTHERS DON'T DRESS ALIKE?
NOPE.

OR HAVE THREE OF EVERYTHING?
NOPE. UNLESS THEY WANT THREE OF SOMETHING INEXPENSIVE.

HOW COME YOU THOUGHT IT WAS SO NEAT THAT MARILYN AND I ARE LOOK-ALIKES AND HAVE ALL THE SAME THINGS?

HUH?

REMEMBER THAT FIRST DAY WHEN YOU SAT FOR US?
IN THE BEGINNING, YOU TRIED TO TELL US APART, BUT THEN YOU WERE JUST LIKE EVERYONE ELSE.
YOU SAID HOW CUTE WE WERE IN OUR MATCHING OUTFITS AND STUFF. WE DECIDED WE WEREN'T GOING TO BE NICE TO BABY-SITTERS ANYMORE AFTER THAT.
SO **THAT** HAD BEEN MY MISTAKE.

I'M SORRY. I REALLY AM.

I DIDN'T MEAN THAT I DIDN'T CARE ABOUT WHO YOU WERE. I JUST MEANT THAT YOU WERE CUTE.

THEN WE'RE SORRY, TOO. WE DIDN'T UNDERSTAND.
YEAH, WE'RE SORRY, TOO.

YOU KNOW, I'VE BEEN THINKING. WOULD YOU LIKE TO TALK TO YOUR MOTHER ABOUT HOW YOU FEEL? I COULD HELP YOU.

TALK TO HER ABOUT WHAT?
ABOUT YOU TWO.

ABOUT LETTING YOU BE INDIVIDUALS.

IF YOU COULD WEAR ANY CLOTHES YOU WANTED, WHAT WOULD THEY LOOK LIKE?

OH, I'D LIKE TO BE MORE GROWN UP! LIKE MORE TOPS AND SKIRTS INSTEAD OF CUTESY DRESSES AND HAIR BOWS.
I'D LIKE TO BE MORE COOL. JEANS AND PUSH-DOWN SOCKS AND BARRETTES WITH RIBBONS ON THEM.
YOU SEE?

YOU LIKE DIFFERENT THINGS. IT ISN'T THAT YOU DON'T WANT TO DRESS THE SAME ANYMORE, YOU JUST WANT TO DRESS LIKE **YOU**.

AND YOU'LL HELP US TALK TO OUR MOM?

HOW ABOUT IT?

YES!

WHEN MRS. ARNOLD CAME HOME, I ASKED IF THE FOUR OF US COULD TALK.
I BECAME A NERVOUS WRECK AS I THOUGHT MORE ABOUT IT. WHAT RIGHT DID I HAVE BUTTING INTO THEIR FAMILY'S BUSINESS?
SO, UM... UH...
MRS. ARNOLD, DID YOU KNOW THAT THREE OF MY BROTHERS ARE TRIPLETS?

NO, I DIDN'T --

AND THEY DON'T HAVE BRACELETS!
AND THEY DRESS DIFFERENTLY! EVERYONE CAN TELL THEM APART!
EVEN THOUGH THEY'RE IDENTICAL.

OH...?

WELL, THE THING IS, I THINK MARILYN AND CAROLYN WOULD LIKE TO BE --
DIFFERENT!

BUT WE LOOK AND DRESS ALIKE, SO EVERYONE TREATS US LIKE ONE PERSON -- THE SAME PERSON.
AND WE AREN'T ONE PERSON, MOMMY!

WE'RE TWO. AND NO ONE KNOWS IT.
AT SCHOOL THE KIDS CALL BOTH OF US MARILYN-OR-CAROLYN.

WE HATE IT!
IF WE WENT TO SCHOOL LOOKING DIFFERENT...
MAYBE THE KIDS WOULD GET TO KNOW WHO WE ARE.
OH, GOOD LINE.
GIRLS, I NEVER REALIZED...
YOU'RE SO ADORABLE IN YOUR MATCHING OUTFITS. I ALWAYS ASSUMED THAT SINCE YOUR FATHER AND I LIKED THE WAY YOU LOOKED, YOU LIKED THE WAY YOU LOOKED.
PLUS, WHEN YOU WERE LITTLE YOU LIKED LOOKING IDENTICAL, DIDN'T YOU?
YES, BUT WE'RE NOT BABIES ANYMORE. WE CAN CHOOSE OUR OWN CLOTHES NOW.

CAN WE COME SHOPPING WITH YOU AND PICK OUT THE THINGS WE LIKE?

OF COURSE! I'D LIKE THAT.

CAN I GROW MY HAIR OUT?
CAN I GET MINE CUT?
OH, YOU TWO...

MALLORY, THANK YOU. I KNOW IT WASN'T EASY TO BRING THIS TO MY ATTENTION.
IT WASN'T, BUT I REALLY LIKE MARILYN AND CAROLYN. I'M GLAD IT WORKED OUT.

MOMMY, CAN WE USE THE MONEY WE GOT ON OUR BIRTHDAY TO BUY NEW CLOTHES?
YES, IT'S YOUR MONEY.
CAN I TAKE THEM SHOPPING ON THURSDAY? MAYBE YOU COULD DROP US OFF DOWNTOWN ON YOUR WAY TO SCHOOL AND PICK US UP AFTERWARD.
PLEAAAAASE!
IT'S A DATE.
YAAAAAAAY!

CHAPTER 12

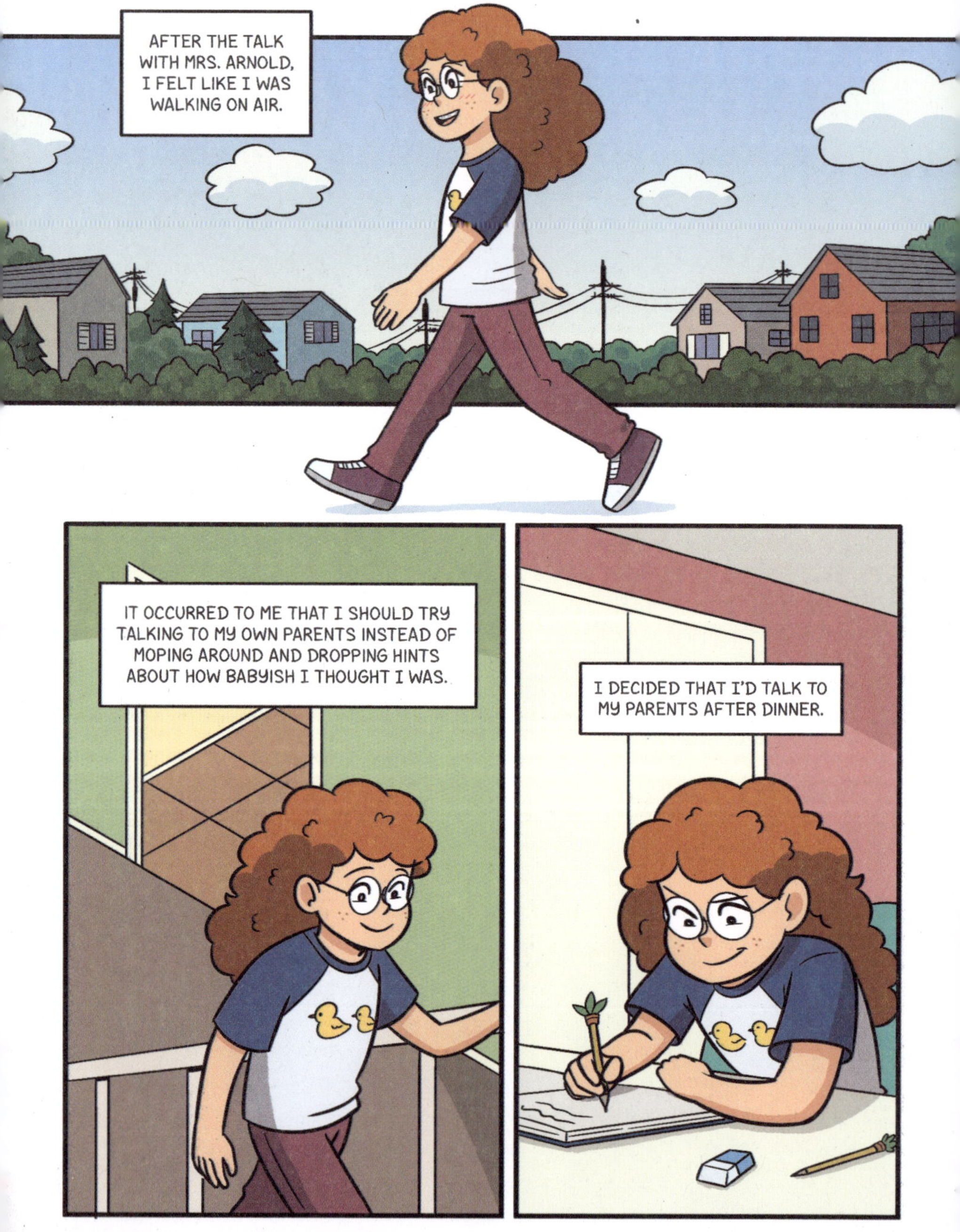

AFTER THE TALK WITH MRS. ARNOLD, I FELT LIKE I WAS WALKING ON AIR.

I HELPFULLY VOLUNTEERED TO CLEAN UP THE TABLE AND KITCHEN.
I EVEN MADE COFFEE FOR MOM AND DAD.
OH, MALLORY, YOU'RE A LIFESAVER.
THANKS, HONEY.
YOU'RE WELCOME.
CAN I TALK TO YOU ABOUT SOMETHING?

MY PARENTS LOOKED LIKE THEY HAD FIGURED EVERYTHING OUT. THEIR EYES SAID, "OH, SO THAT'S WHY SHE WAS BEING SO HELPFUL AFTER DINNER."

THEY MUST BE WIZARDS.

SO, UH, MOM, DAD, I'M ELEVEN YEARS OLD. SOON I'LL BE TWELVE.

OH BOY. THEN AFTER THAT YOU'LL BE A TEENAGER.
PAT
PAT
EXACTLY.

I'M NOT A KID ANYMORE. BUT I FEEL LIKE ONE.

I HAVE THIS MESSY HAIR... AND MY CLOTHES ARE NICE, BUT THEY'RE YOUNG AND BABYISH.
AND I WOULD LIKE TO GET MY EARS PIERCED.
OH, AND CONTACT LENSES. I'D REALLY LIKE CONTACT LENSES.
THAT'S ALL I WANT -- A HAIRCUT, PIERCED EARS, CONTACT LENSES, AND A BRAND-NEW WARDROBE.
WHAT?
YOU WANT **WHAT?**
A HAIRCUT, PIERCED EARS, CONTACT LENSES, AND A NEW WARDROBE.

HMM. LET'S TRY TURNING IT UP A NOTCH.

UGH...

I'M SUCH A BABY!!!

OH, HONEY...
YOU'RE NOT A BABY.
YOU'RE ALSO NOT OLD ENOUGH TO GET CONTACT LENSES.

AND I'M AFRAID WE CAN'T AFFORD A NEW WARDROBE FOR YOU.
DO YOU HAVE ANY IDEA HOW MUCH THAT WOULD COST?

NO. HOW MUCH?
I DID KNOW, THOUGH. THE WARDROBE WAS ONE OF MY BARGAINING CHIPS. I WASN'T EXPECTING TO GET IT, SO I COULD EASILY GIVE IT UP.

A LOT. IT WOULD COST A LOT.
OH...

I DON'T SEE WHY YOU COULDN'T GET YOUR HAIR CUT, THOUGH.

COULD YOU PAY FOR HALF OF IT WITH YOUR BABY-SITTING MONEY?
SURE!

ALL RIGHT. THEN YOU MAY GET YOUR HAIR CUT. ON ONE CONDITION.

THAT YOU DON'T GO TO THAT PLACE WHERE YOU'LL COME OUT WITH A NEON GREEN MOHAWK. I WANT YOU TO GO TO THE SALON DOWNTOWN.
DEAL.

AND WHAT ABOUT PIERCED EARS?

EARRINGS LOOK SO PRETTY, AND I PROMISE I WON'T GET MORE THAN ONE HOLE IN EACH EAR OR ANYTHING WEIRD LIKE, YOU KNOW, SNAKE FANGS.
I'LL JUST WEAR LITTLE GOLD DOTS, OR MAYBE GOLD HOOPS, BUT TINY ONES.

PLEASE, PLEASE, PLEASE, PLEASE, **PLEASE** CAN I GET THEM PIERCED?

HMM. I WAS TWELVE WHEN I GOT MY EARS PIERCED. YOU'RE PRETTY CLOSE TO TWELVE.

WHAT DO YOU THINK?

I SUPPOSE IT'S ALL RIGHT -- IF IT'S OKAY WITH YOU.

IT'S OKAY WITH ME ON THREE CONDITIONS.
NOW IT'S THREE? WHAT ARE THEY?

ONE, THAT YOU PAY FOR THE EAR PIERCING AND EARRINGS YOURSELF.
OKAY.

TWO, THAT YOU DO EVERYTHING YOU'RE TOLD TO PREVENT INFECTED EARS. **EVERYTHING.**
ALL RIGHT.

AND THREE...

THAT YOU **DON'T** STICK TO TINY GOLD EARRINGS. WHAT'S THE POINT IN HAVING PIERCED EARS IF YOU CAN'T WEAR SNAKE FANGS EVERY NOW AND THEN?

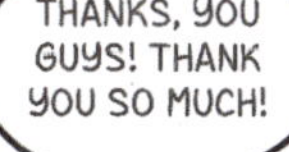
THANKS, YOU GUYS! THANK YOU SO MUCH!

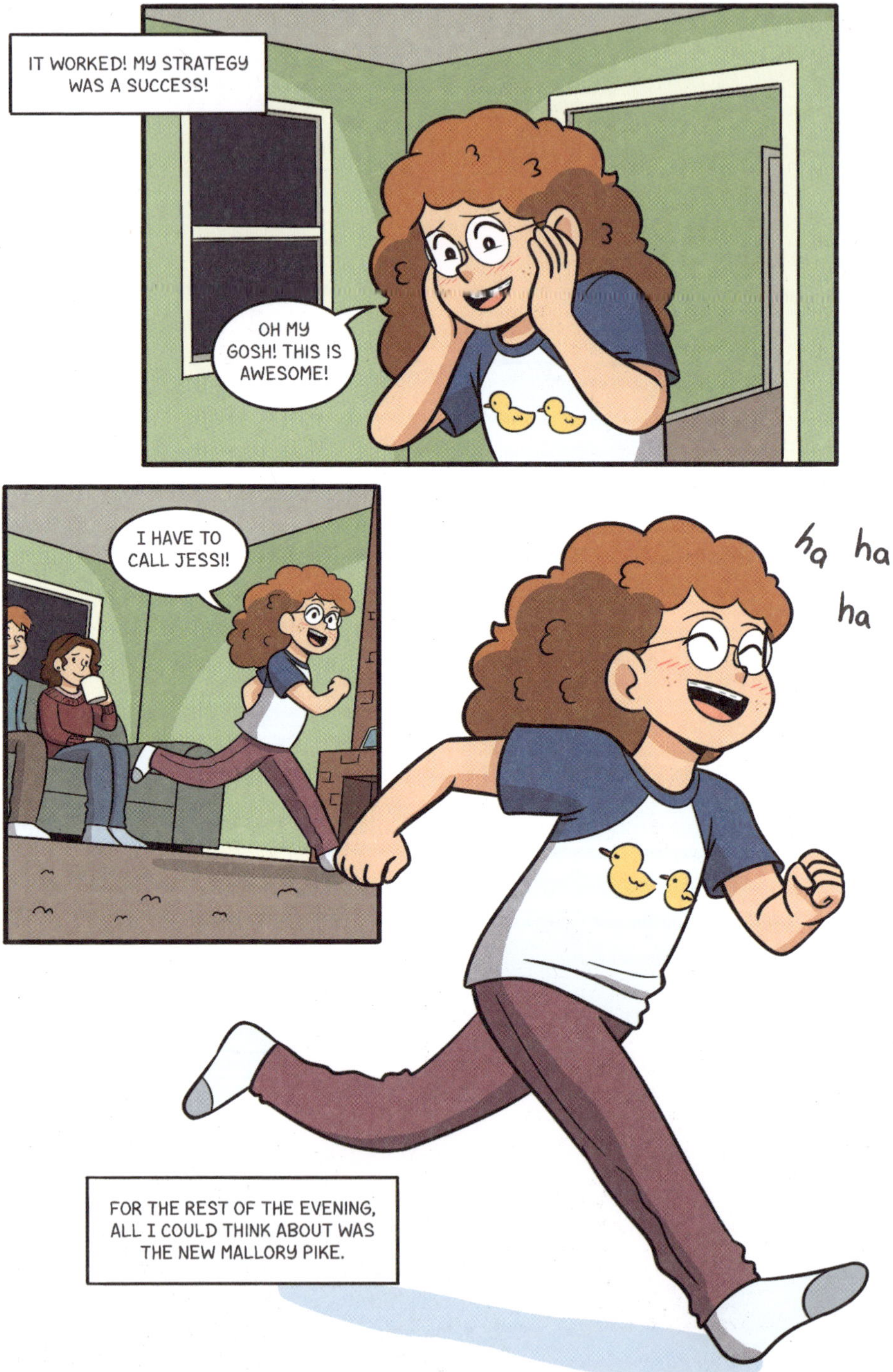

I HAVE TO CALL JESSI!

ha ha ha

FOR THE REST OF THE EVENING, ALL I COULD THINK ABOUT WAS THE NEW MALLORY PIKE.

CHAPTER 13

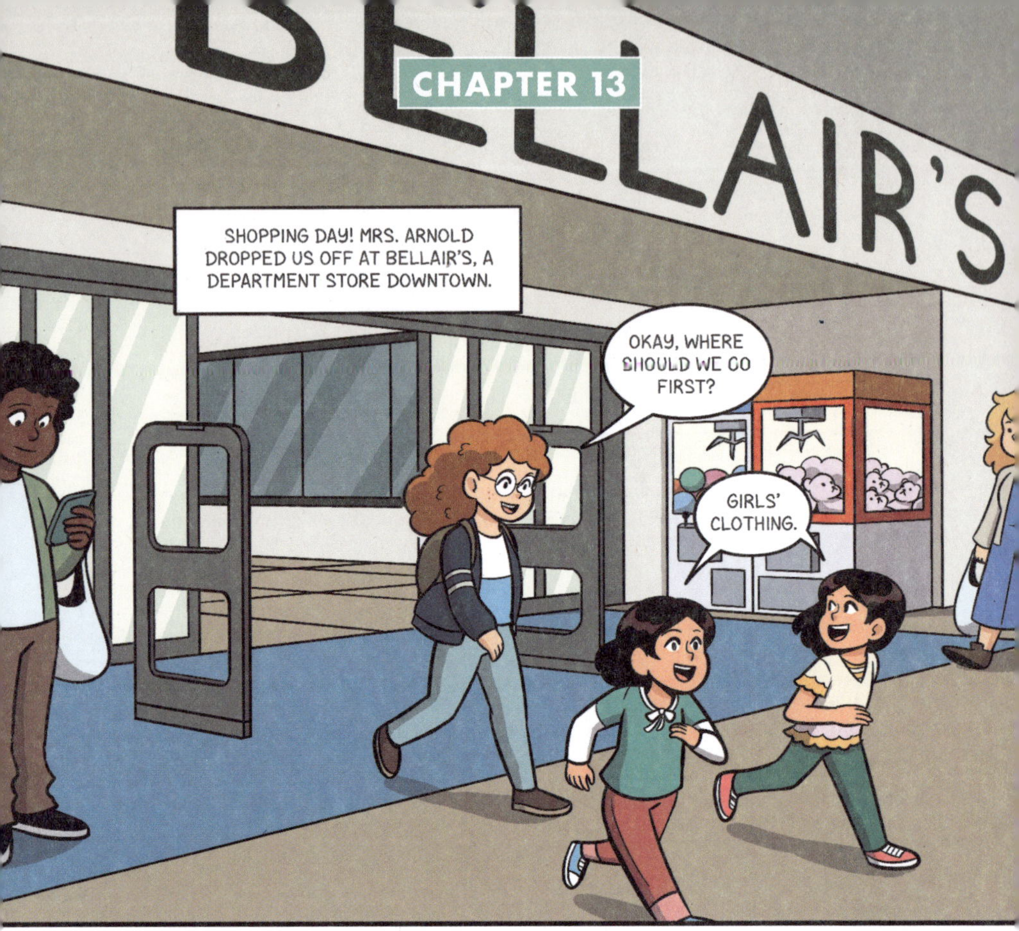

BELLAIR'S

SHOPPING DAY! MRS. ARNOLD DROPPED US OFF AT BELLAIR'S, A DEPARTMENT STORE DOWNTOWN.

OKAY, WHERE SHOULD WE GO FIRST?

GIRLS' CLOTHING.

HOP
THUD

WE HAVE A PLAN.
YUP. CLOTHES ARE EXPENSIVE AND WE DON'T HAVE A LOT OF BIRTHDAY MONEY.

WE WANT TO BE CAREFUL TODAY. WE WANT TO SEE WHAT WE LIKE AT THE STORES --
AND HOW MUCH THINGS COST. THEN, WE'LL DECIDE WHAT TO BUY AND GO BACK AND GET THEM.

THAT MAKES SENSE TO ME.
OOOOOOOH!

THIS IS SOOO PRETTY!

LET'S SEE HOW MUCH IT --
$135.00

WE WENT TO A FEW DIFFERENT STORES IN THE AREA.
3
4
Cozeez

MERRY-GO-ROUND

whew...
WE HAVE TO MEET YOUR MOM IN LESS THAN AN HOUR, SO I THINK YOU BETTER DECIDE WHAT YOU WANT TO BUY, AND THEN WE CAN GO BACK AND GET THE THINGS.
ARE YOU READY TO DO THAT?
I THINK SO.
WE JUST NEED TO ADD UP ALL THE PRICES.
LET ME HELP YOU DO SOME MATH.

AFTER MUCH DISCUSSION, WE WENT BACK TO EACH STORE AND PURCHASED MARILYN'S AND CAROLYN'S ITEMS.
THE GRINS ON BOTH GIRLS' FACES WERE AT LEAST A MILE WIDE!
ALL OUR MONEY IS GONE, BUT WE DON'T CARE.
YEAH, WE'RE SO LUCKY.
FROM NOW ON, WHEN MOMMY GOES SHOPPING, WE'LL GO WITH HER. NO MORE YUCKY OUTFITS!
TWENTY MINUTES UNTIL YOUR MOM WILL BE BACK. WHAT DO YOU WANT TO DO?
LET'S PUT ON OUR NEW CLOTHES!

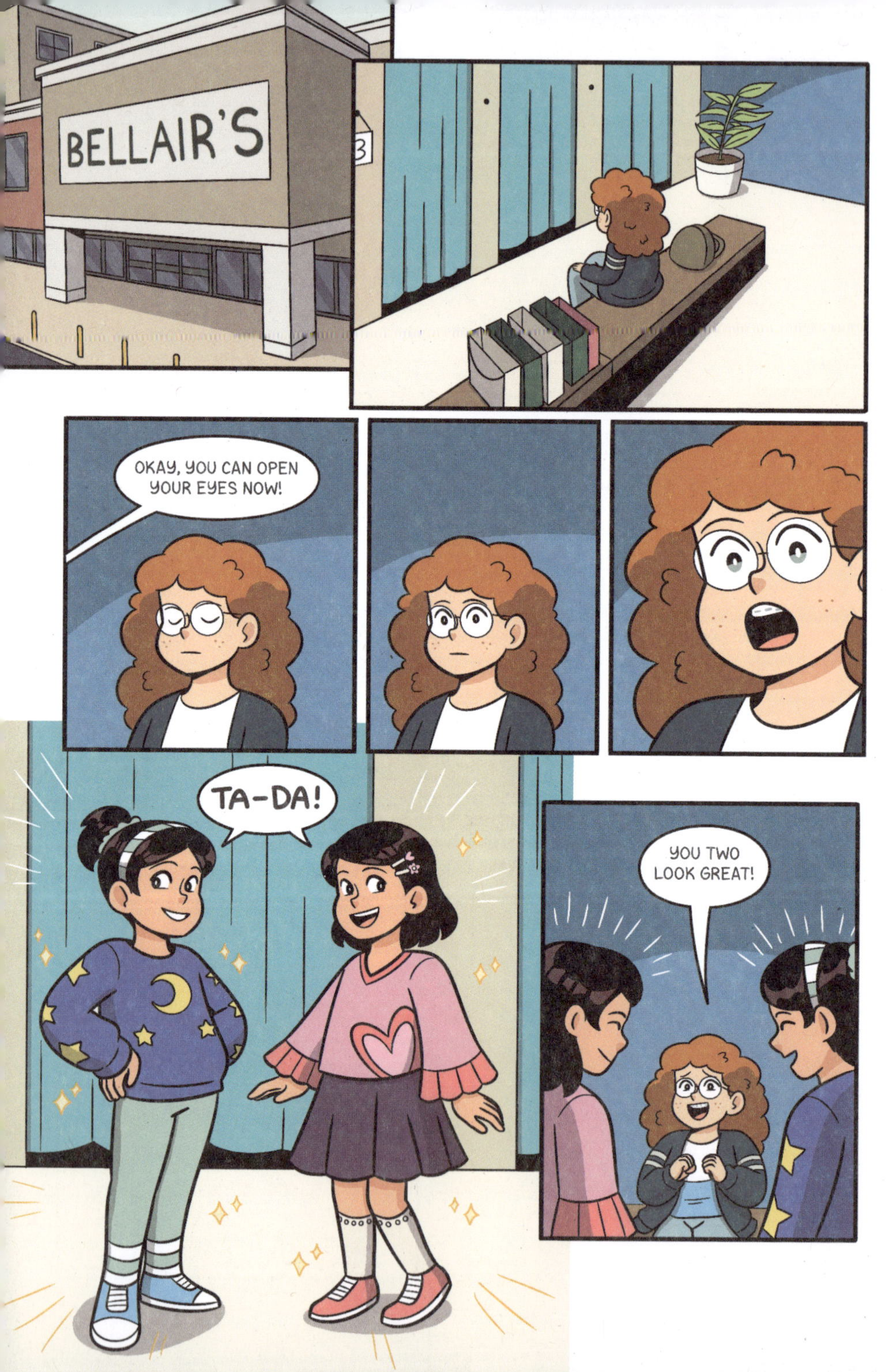
BELLAIR'S
3
OKAY, YOU CAN OPEN YOUR EYES NOW!
TA-DA!
YOU TWO LOOK GREAT!

I WISHED I HAD A CAMERA TO CAPTURE MRS. ARNOLD'S REACTIONS TO HER DAUGHTERS' NEW APPEARANCES.

AT FIRST SHE WAS SHOCKED...

THEN AMAZED...

AND FINALLY, PLEASED.

MY STEADY JOB WITH THE ARNOLDS WOULD BE OVER SOON, BUT I HOPED THEY WOULD NEED ME AGAIN IN THE FUTURE.
I'D TAKE CARE OF THE TROUBLESOME TWINS ANY DAY.

CHAPTER 14

GUESS WHAT, GUESS WHAT, GUESS WHAT!
WHAT?
MY PARENTS SAID I CAN GET MY EARS PIERCED!
OH MY GOSH! THAT'S AMAZING! WE CAN GO TOGETHER!

YES!!!

AT THE NEXT BSC MEETING, JESSI AND I TOLD THE OTHER GIRLS OUR NEWS.

HA HA! OH, YOU WON'T BELIEVE THIS.
IT MUST BE EAR-PIERCING SEASON IN STONEYBROOK.
I JUST GOT PERMISSION TO GET ANOTHER HOLE IN MY RIGHT EAR!
YOU'RE KIDDING!

THEN WE SHOULD ALL HAVE THEM DONE AT THE SAME TIME!

HEY, I'VE GOT AN IDEA.

WE HAVEN'T HAD A CLUB PARTY IN A WHILE. INSTEAD OF ONE, HOW ABOUT WE PAY CHARLIE TO DRIVE US TO WASHINGTON MALL NEXT WEEKEND?
YOU THREE COULD GET YOUR EARS PIERCED AND THEN WE CAN WALK AROUND THE MALL.

OKAY!

FIVE DAYS LATER, CHARLIE THOMAS DROPPED US OFF AT WASHINGTON MALL.
WASHINGTON MALL
I WAS SO EXCITED, I COULD HEAR MY HEART POUNDING.
Beverley BEAUTY
RT
3

Ear Piercing Boutique
I'M GETTING SCARED.
IT'S OKAY. WE'RE DOING THIS TOGETHER!
THE PIERCING WILL BE OVER QUICKLY AND YOU WON'T FEEL A THING!
WELL, ACTUALLY, IT DEPENDS ON YOUR PAIN TOLERANCE, BUT I'M SURE YOU'LL BE --
OOPS. I'LL STOP TALKING NOW...

HEY, CHEER UP! THIS IS FUN!

WE'RE MALLING, YOU GUYS! WE'VE NEVER DONE THIS AS A CLUB!

MALLING. IT HAD A NICE RING TO IT.
ha
ha
ha

Ear Piercing Boutique

HELLO! MAY I HELP YOU?
SUE

HELLO. THE THREE OF US WOULD LIKE TO GET OUR EARS PIERCED, PLEASE.
GREAT.
WHO WANTS TO GO FIRST?
SUE

GO ON, MAL. EAR-PIERCING WAS YOUR IDEA.
ha
ha
ha

I COULDN'T BELIEVE IT. I WAS FINALLY SITTING IN ONE OF THE STOOLS!

I'VE MARKED WHERE THE HOLES WILL GO. DOES THIS LOOK GOOD TO YOU?
YUP. PERFECT.
SUE

WE'RE READY TO GO, THEN.
SUE

POKE
PRESS
POKE
PRESS

ALL DONE!
SUE

WHOA.

I HAD DONE IT! MY EARS SHINED WITH ACTUAL EARRINGS!

I FELT INCREDIBLY COOL!
AWESOME!
THEY LOOK GREAT ON YOU!
CONGRATS, MAL!
THANKS, GUYS!

JESSI WAS NEXT.

PLEASE HOLD MY HAND.

NO PROBLEM.

POKE
PRESS
POKE
PRESS

DONE.

REALLY? THAT WASN'T BAD AT ALL!
SUE

CLAUDIA WAS LAST.
SHE LOOKED AS IF SHE WAS IN A RESTAURANT, WAITING FOR SOMEONE TO TAKE HER ORDER.
POKE
PRESS
SUE
THANKS!
SINK
I CAN'T BELIEVE I ALMOST PASSED OUT.
SUE

ONCE CLAUDIA WAS FEELING BETTER, WE LEARNED HOW TO CARE FOR OUR EARS AND PAID. THEN WE WENT MALLING FOR A COUPLE HOURS.

FINALLY, WE HEADED TO THE MALL ENTRANCE WHERE CHARLIE WAS SUPPOSED TO PICK US UP.
WEAR
I WAS HAPPY I HAD TAKEN THE FIRST BIG STEP TOWARD BECOMING THE NEW MALLORY PIKE.

CHAPTER 15

ONE MONTH LATER
Downtown Do
HAIRCUT DAY!
OPEN

I DIDN'T KNOW EXACTLY WHAT I WANTED DONE. LUCKILY, AMBER, MY HAIRDRESSER, WAS VERY UNDERSTANDING.

HERE ARE SOME PICTURES. SEE WHAT YOU LIKE. THEN I'LL TELL YOU IF I CAN DO IT TO YOUR HAIR.

HMMM...

THIS ONE. THIS ONE. OR THIS ONE.
OKAY...

NOW **THAT'S** ONE YOUR HAIR IS PERFECT FOR.
WHEN WE CUT YOUR HAIR, YOUR CURLS WILL RELAX INTO THOSE WAVES.

TWO DAYS LATER...
ORDER, ORDER.

WELL, LET'S SEE...
UM, HAS EVERYONE READ THE CLUB NOTEBOOK?

YES.

OKAY, WELL, UM...

ANY BUSINESS TO DISCUSS?

KRISTY, IS EVERYTHING ALL RIGHT?

OH, SURE. WHY?

YOU SEEM... I DON'T KNOW.

WELL, I'M FINE.
OKAY.

DARN IT! I CAN'T STAND IT ANY LONGER!
MARY ANNE, IT'S TIME FOR --

RiNG

HELLO?
OKAY. WE'LL GET BACK TO YOU.

THAT WAS MRS. ARNOLD. SHE NEEDS A SITTER FOR THE TWINS NEXT THURSDAY AFTERNOON.

LET'S SEE...

GOSH, THREE OF US ARE FREE. KRISTY, DAWN, AND ME.

HEY, MAL, HOW **ARE** THE TWINS THESE DAYS? I KNOW YOU ENDED UP LIKING THEM, BUT...

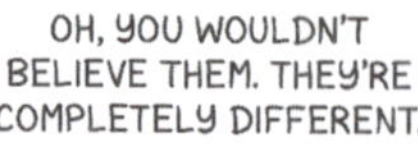
OH, YOU WOULDN'T BELIEVE THEM. THEY'RE COMPLETELY DIFFERENT.

MRS. ARNOLD FINALLY LET CAROLYN GET HER HAIR CUT AND MARILYN IS GROWING HERS OUT.
THEY NEVER DRESS THE SAME ANYMORE AND EVERYONE CAN TELL THEM APART, SO THEY'RE MUCH HAPPIER.

WHICHEVER ONE OF YOU GETS THE JOB WILL BE REALLY PLEASED.
THEY'RE NOT TROUBLESOME TWINS ANYMORE.

ALL RIGHT. I'M CONVINCED. I'LL TAKE IT.

NOW AS I
WAS SAYING --

RING

THREE MORE CALLS
CAME IN, ONE RIGHT
AFTER THE OTHER.

CLICK

OKAY, **NOW,** MARY ANNE AND I HAVE SOME SURPRISES.

SURPRISES?

YUP!
THESE ARE FROM KRISTY AND ME. THEY'RE PRESENTS IN HONOR OF YOUR NEW EAR PIERCINGS!

OH, WOW!
THIS IS SO NICE OF YOU! THANKS!
WHAT A COINCIDENCE.
HOLD ON. DON'T OPEN YOUR GIFTS YET.
PULL

I'M GIVING OUT GIFTS, TOO!

OH! WAIT! ONE MORE...

rustle rustle

THIS IS FOR YOU, JESSI.

AW, THANK YOU, MAL.

I'M SORRY I DON'T HAVE SOMETHING FOR EVERYONE.
I GOT THIS A WHILE AGO AND I DIDN'T KNOW THIS MEETING WOULD TURN INTO A GIFT EXCHANGE.
NO WORRIES.

FIRST WE OPENED KRISTY AND MARY ANNE'S GIFTS.
THE EARRINGS THEY BOUGHT WERE VERY THOUGHTFULLY CHOSEN. WE WERE THRILLED!

THANK YOU!!

NEXT WE OPENED CLAUD'S GIFTS.

I MADE THEM MYSELF.

AMAZING!
YOU MADE THESE?
YEP, ALL THE POSTS ARE HYPOALLERGENIC, TOO.
SHE ALSO MADE CLIP-ON EARRINGS FOR KRISTY AND MARY ANNE.
THANKS, CLAUD!
OF COURSE, WE PUT THEM ON IMMEDIATELY!
SAY CHEESE, EVERYONE!
CHEESE!

HEY, JESSI, YOU DIDN'T OPEN --
I KNOW.

FOR SOME REASON, I WANTED TO DO IT IN PRIVATE.

OOH.

BOOKS. JUST LIKE YOURS.
YUP.

SO WE CAN BE TWINS?
ha ha
NO.

BEST FRIENDS.
YEAH, BEST FRIENDS.